P9-DJU-872

THE SATURDAY EVENING POST AMERICANA

COLORING BOOK

RENDERED FOR COLORING BY

MARTY NOBLE

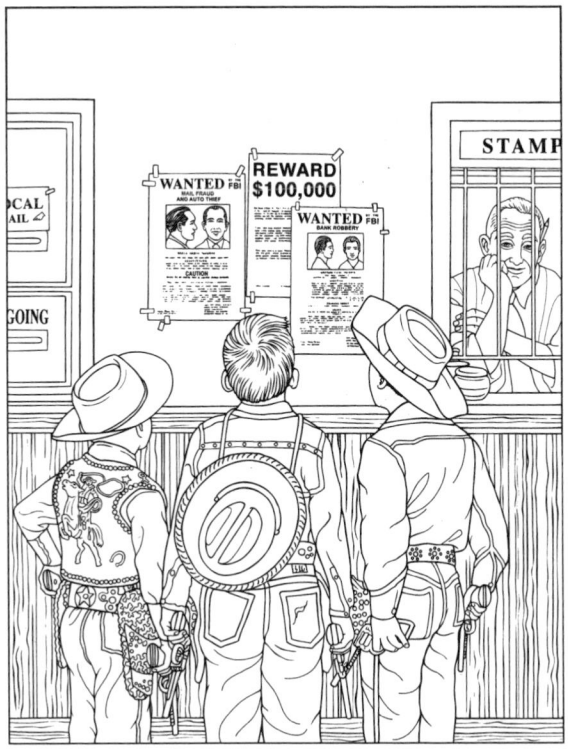

DOVER PUBLICATIONS, INC.
MINEOLA, NEW YORK

It's hard to think of an American publication more iconic than *The Saturday Evening Post,* which has been in print for nearly two hundred years (and possibly has kinship with Benjamin Franklin's *Pennsylvania Gazette,* published in the 1700s). The *Post,* whose first issue appeared on August 4, 1821, has always reflected America's lifestyle, values, and interests. Its content includes feature articles and editorials, short fiction (including stories and poetry by renowned authors such as Edgar Allan Poe, Sinclair Lewis, Dorothy Parker, F. Scott Fitzgerald, and Kurt Vonnegut, Jr.), and cartoons. To many, however, the magazine is forever associated with its covers, many hundreds of which have delighted and moved readers throughout the decades. This unique and delightful coloring book offers an array of coloring opportunities, as you enjoy the illustrations created by some of the *Saturday Evening Post*'s most revered cover artists, among them Stevan Dohanos, John Clymer, George Hughes, and John Falter. Printed on the back of each coloring plate are the cover's title, the name of the artist who created it, and its date of publication. The thirty-one plates have been perforated for removal to make displaying your work easy. Enjoy your adventure into this delicious slice of Americana!

Copyright

Illustrations © SEPS. Licensed by Curtis Licensing, Indianapolis, IN.
All rights reserved.

Bibliographical Note

The Saturday Evening Post Americana Coloring Book is a new work, first published by Dover Publications, Inc., in 2017.

International Standard Book Number

ISBN-13: 978-0-486-81434-6
ISBN-10: 0-486-81434-3

Manufactured in the United States by LSC Communications
81434303 2017
www.doverpublications.com

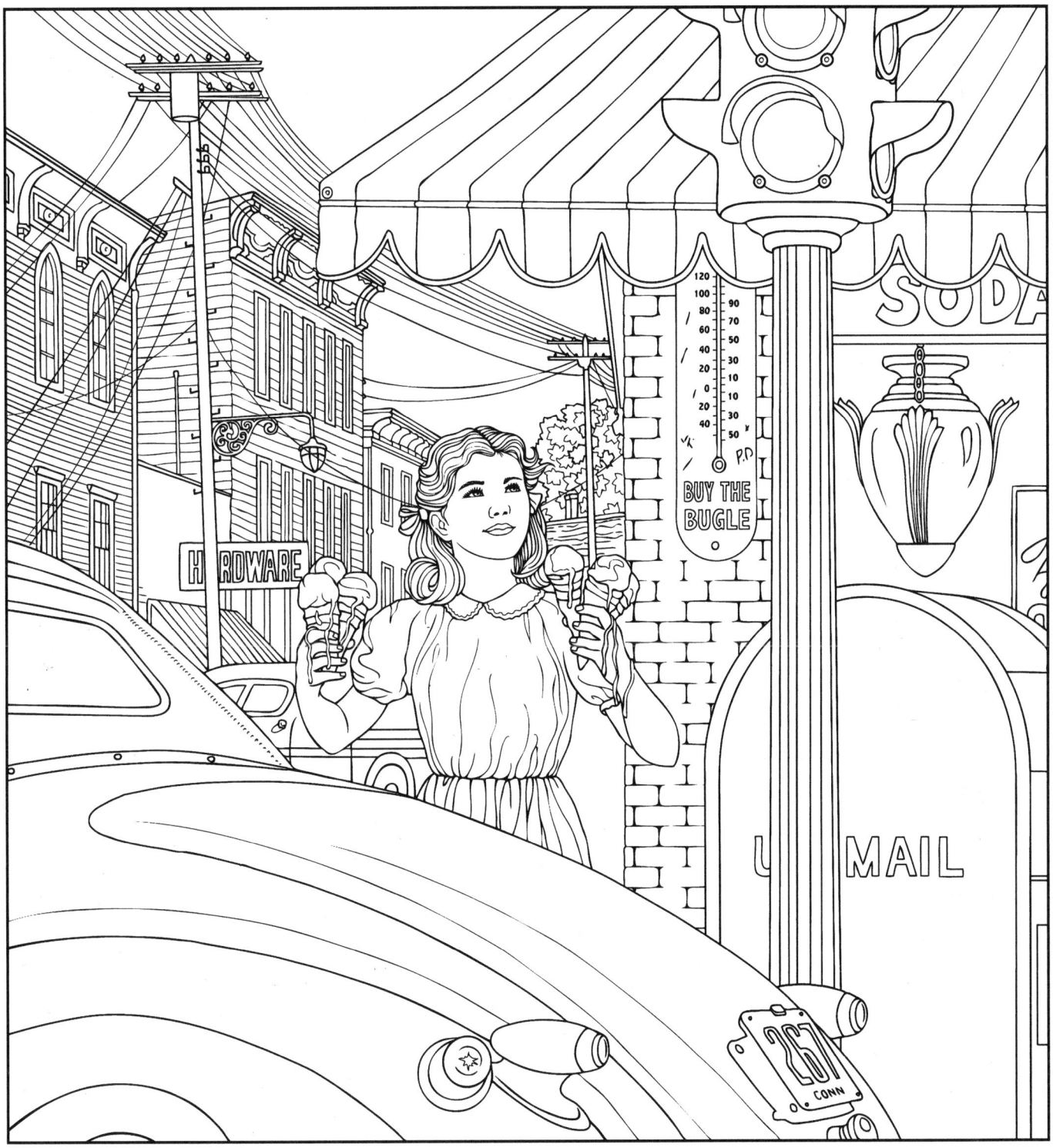
SODA
HARDWARE
BUY THE
BUGLE
MAIL
CONN

PLATE 1
Dripping Cones
Stevan Dohanos
Saturday Evening Post Cover, July 29, 1944
Illustration © SEPS. Licensed by Curtis Licensing, Indianapolis, IN.

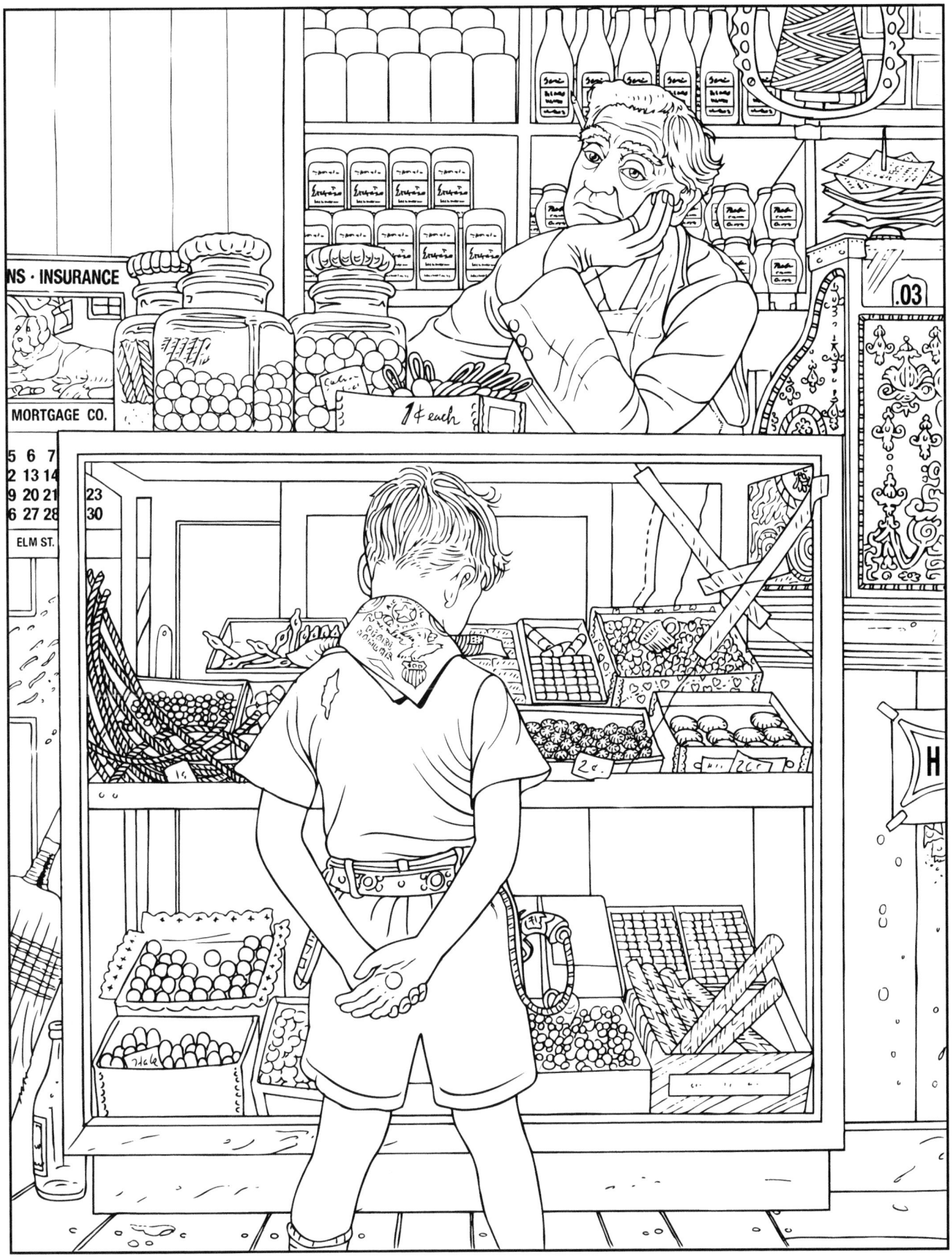
NS · INSURANCE
MORTGAGE CO.
1¢ each
.03
5 6 7
2 13 14
9 20 21
6 27 28
23
30
ELM ST.
1¢
2¢
2¢
H

PLATE 2
Penny Candy
Stevan Dohanos
Saturday Evening Post Cover, September 23, 1944
Illustration © SEPS. Licensed by Curtis Licensing, Indianapolis, IN.

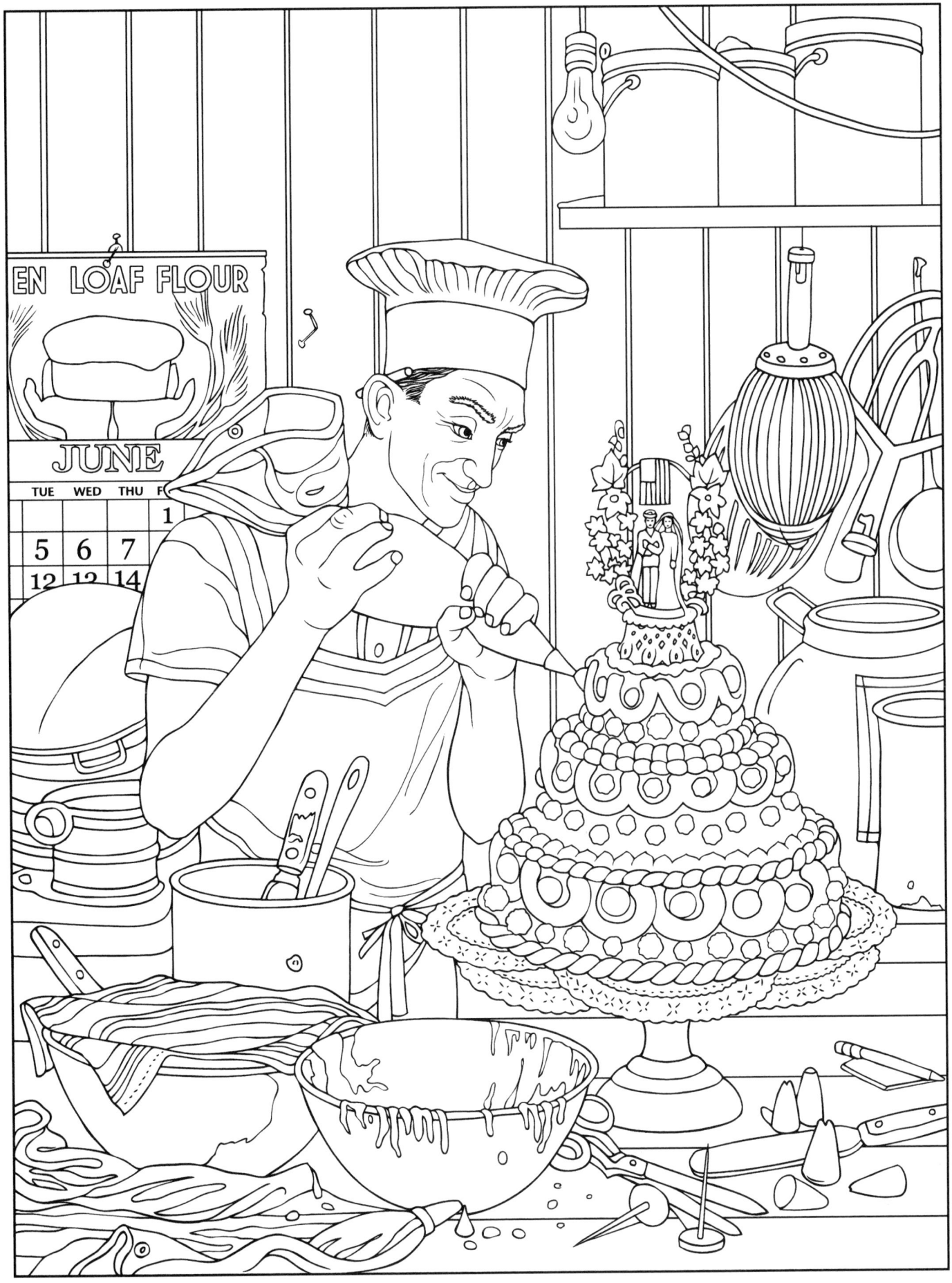
EN LOAF FLOUR
JUNE
TUE WED THU F
1
5 6 7

PLATE 3
Icing the Wedding Cake
Stevan Dohanos
Saturday Evening Post Cover, June 16, 1945
Illustration © SEPS. Licensed by Curtis Licensing, Indianapolis, IN.

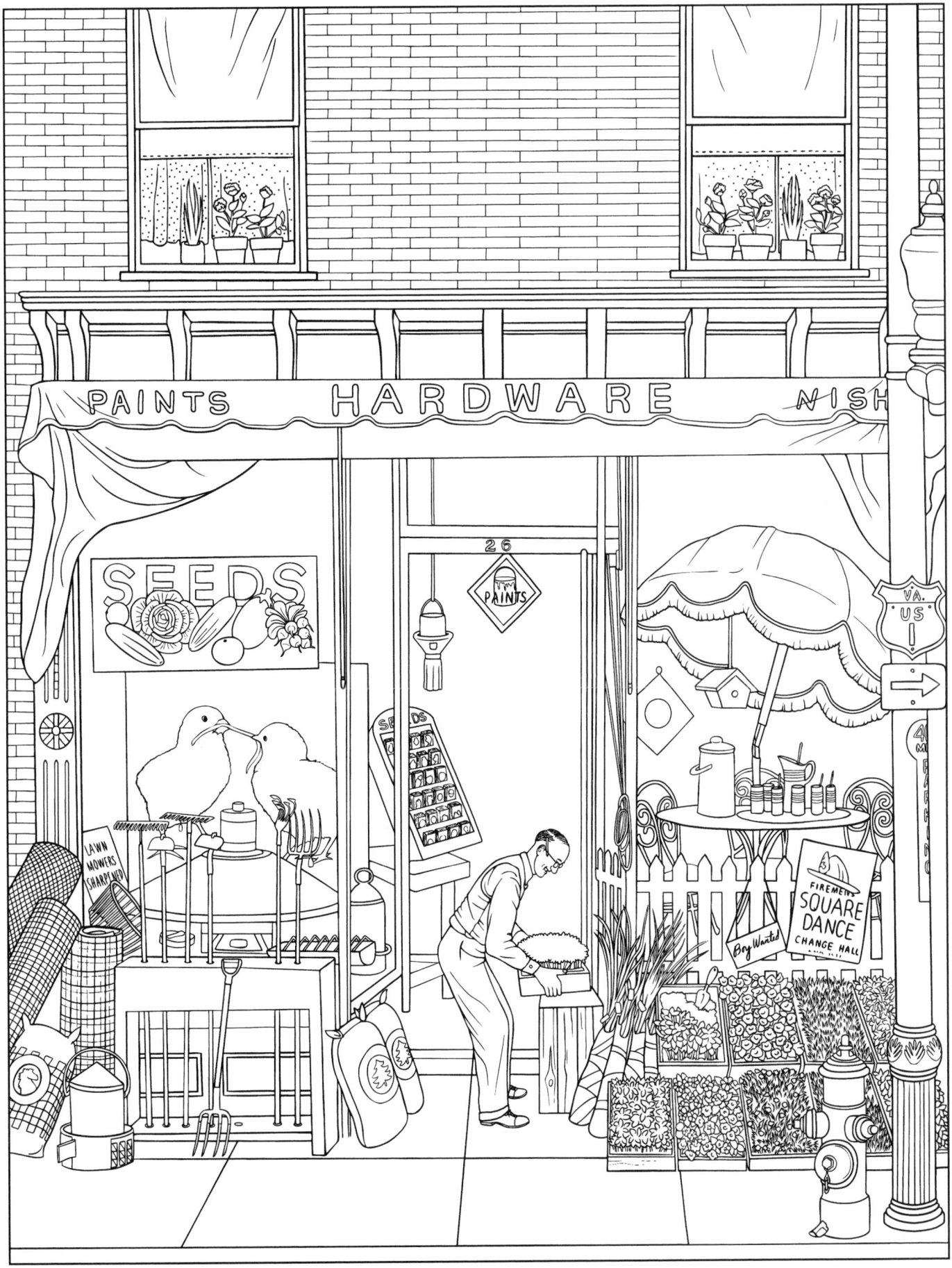
PAINTS
HARDWARE
SEEDS
26
PAINTS
VA.
US
1
LAWN MOWERS SHARPENED
Boy Wanted
FIREMEN'S
SQUARE DANCE
CHANGE HALL

PLATE 4
Hardware Store at Springtime
Stevan Dohanos
Saturday Evening Post Cover, March 16, 1946
Illustration © SEPS. Licensed by Curtis Licensing, Indianapolis, IN.

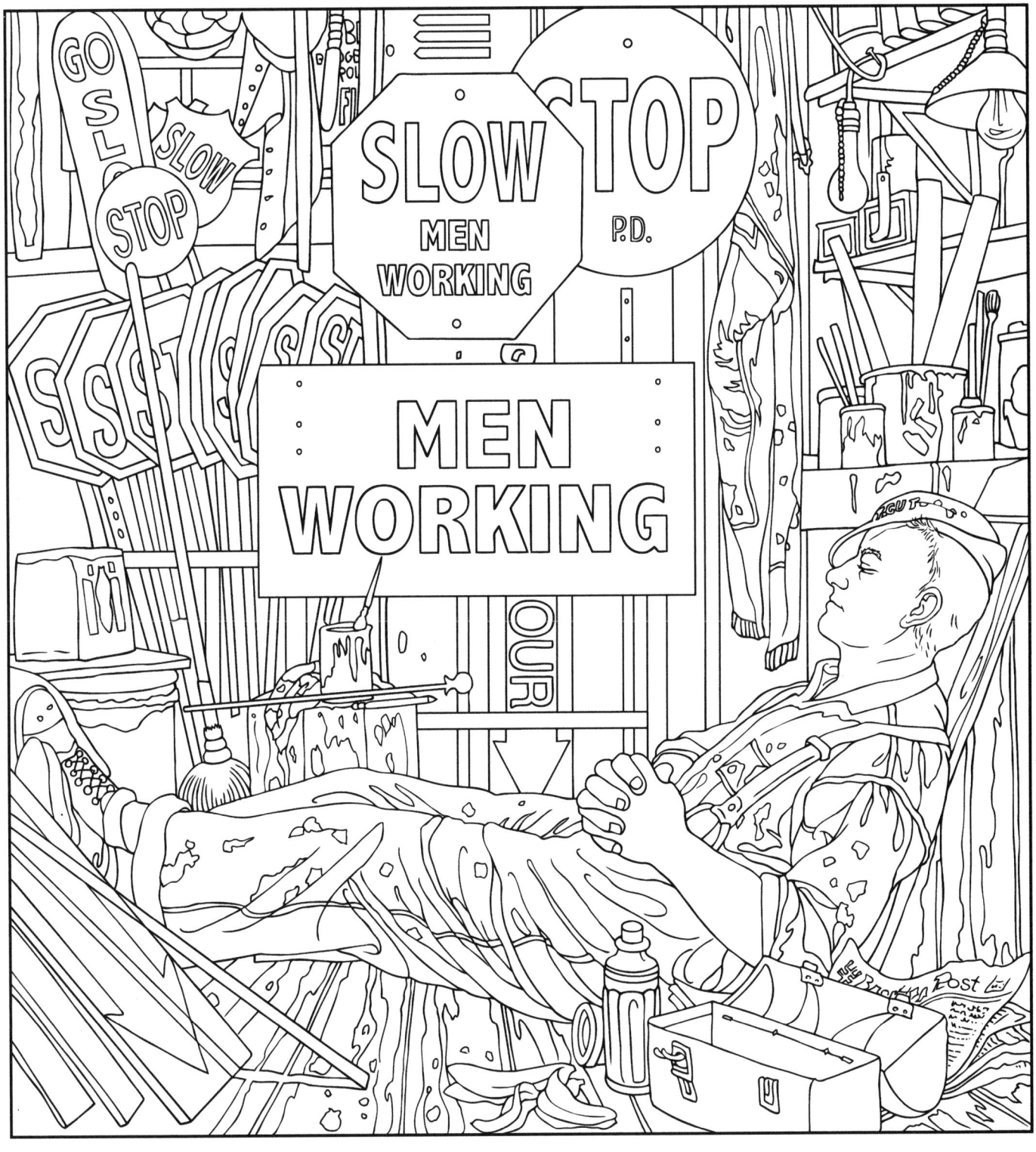
GO
SLOW
STOP
SLOW
MEN
WORKING
STOP
P.D.
MEN
WORKING
OUR
Post

PLATE 5
Men Working
Stevan Dohanos
Saturday Evening Post Cover, April 12, 1947
Illustration © SEPS. Licensed by Curtis Licensing, Indianapolis, IN.

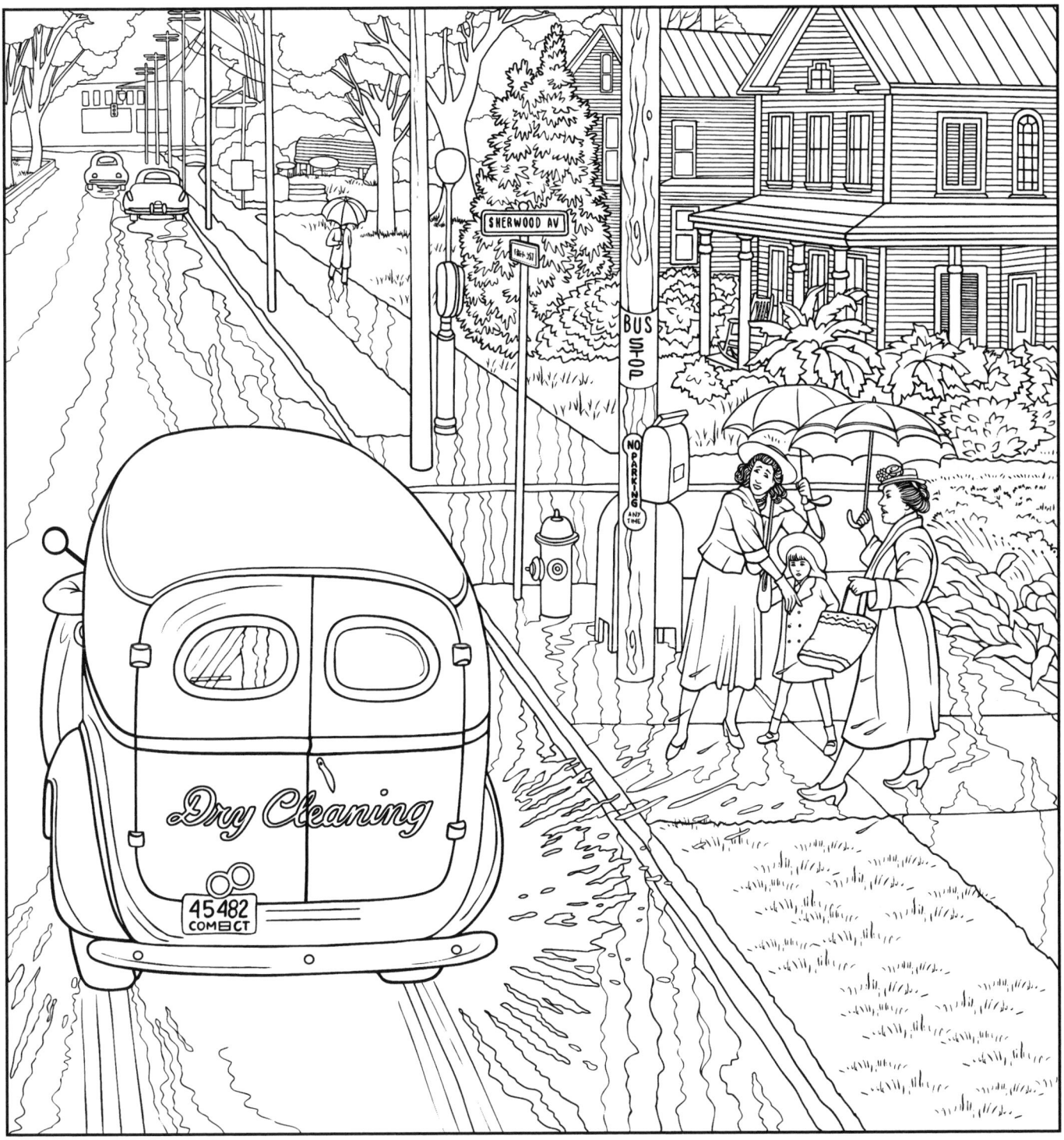
SHERWOOD AV
BUS STOP
NO PARKING ANY TIME
Dry Cleaning
45482
COM CT

PLATE 6
Muddied by Dry Cleaning Truck
Stevan Dohanos
Saturday Evening Post Cover, October 2, 1948
Illustration © SEPS. Licensed by Curtis Licensing, Indianapolis, IN.

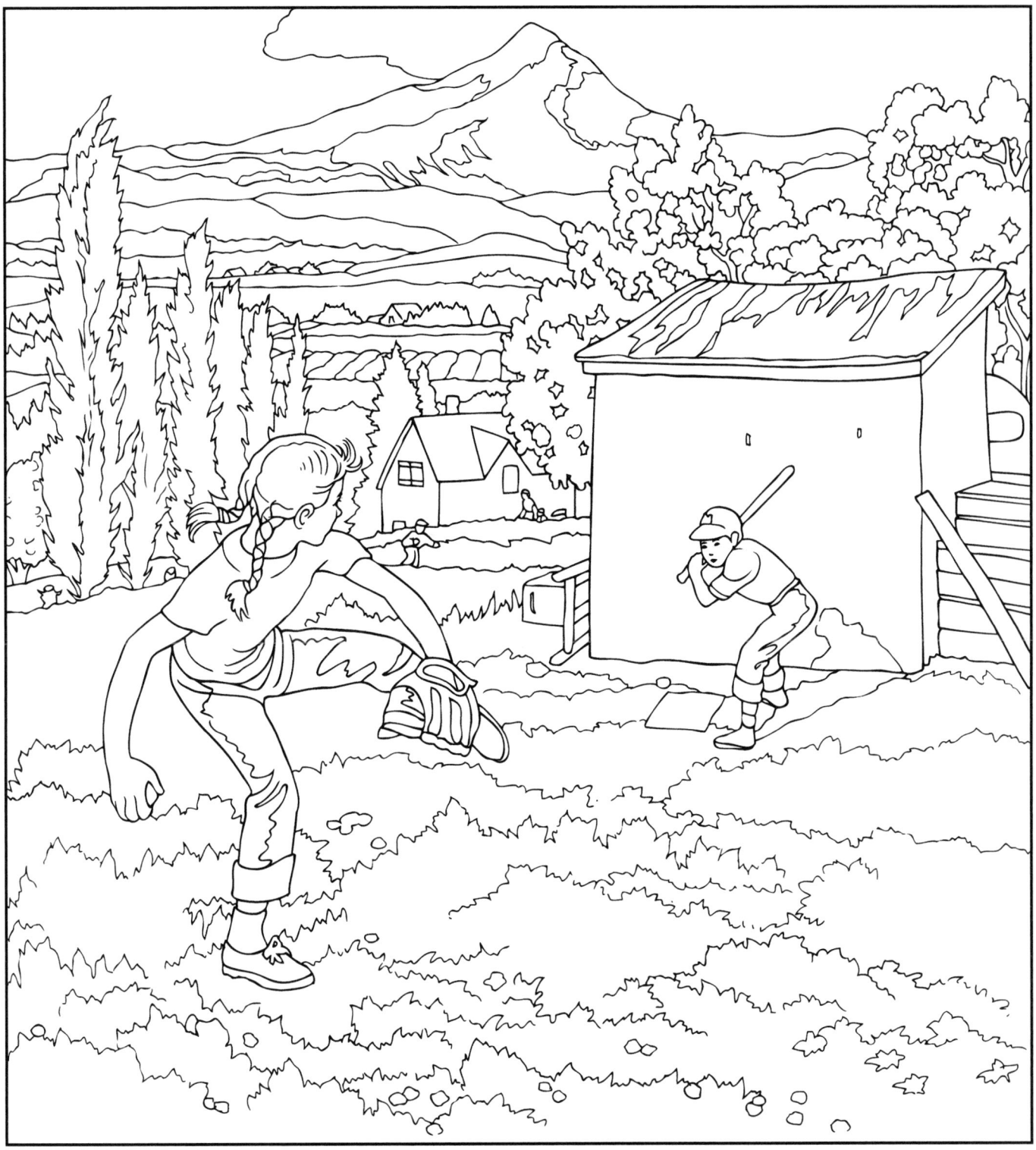

PLATE 7
Oregon Baseball
John Clymer
Saturday Evening Post Cover, April 21, 1951
Illustration © SEPS. Licensed by Curtis Licensing, Indianapolis, IN.

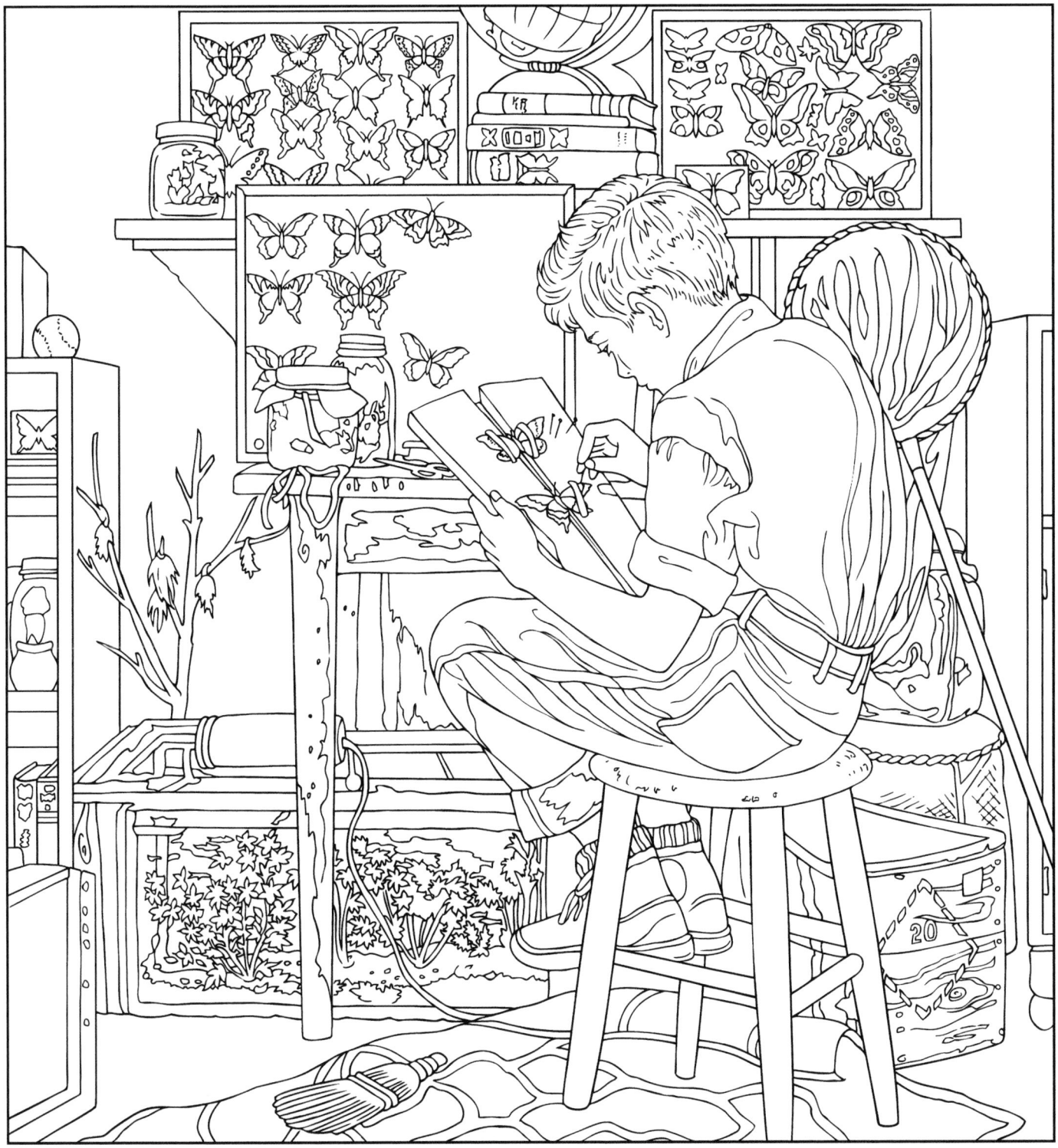
20

PLATE 8
The Collector
Stevan Dohanos
Saturday Evening Post Cover, August 11, 1951
Illustration © SEPS. Licensed by Curtis Licensing, Indianapolis, IN.

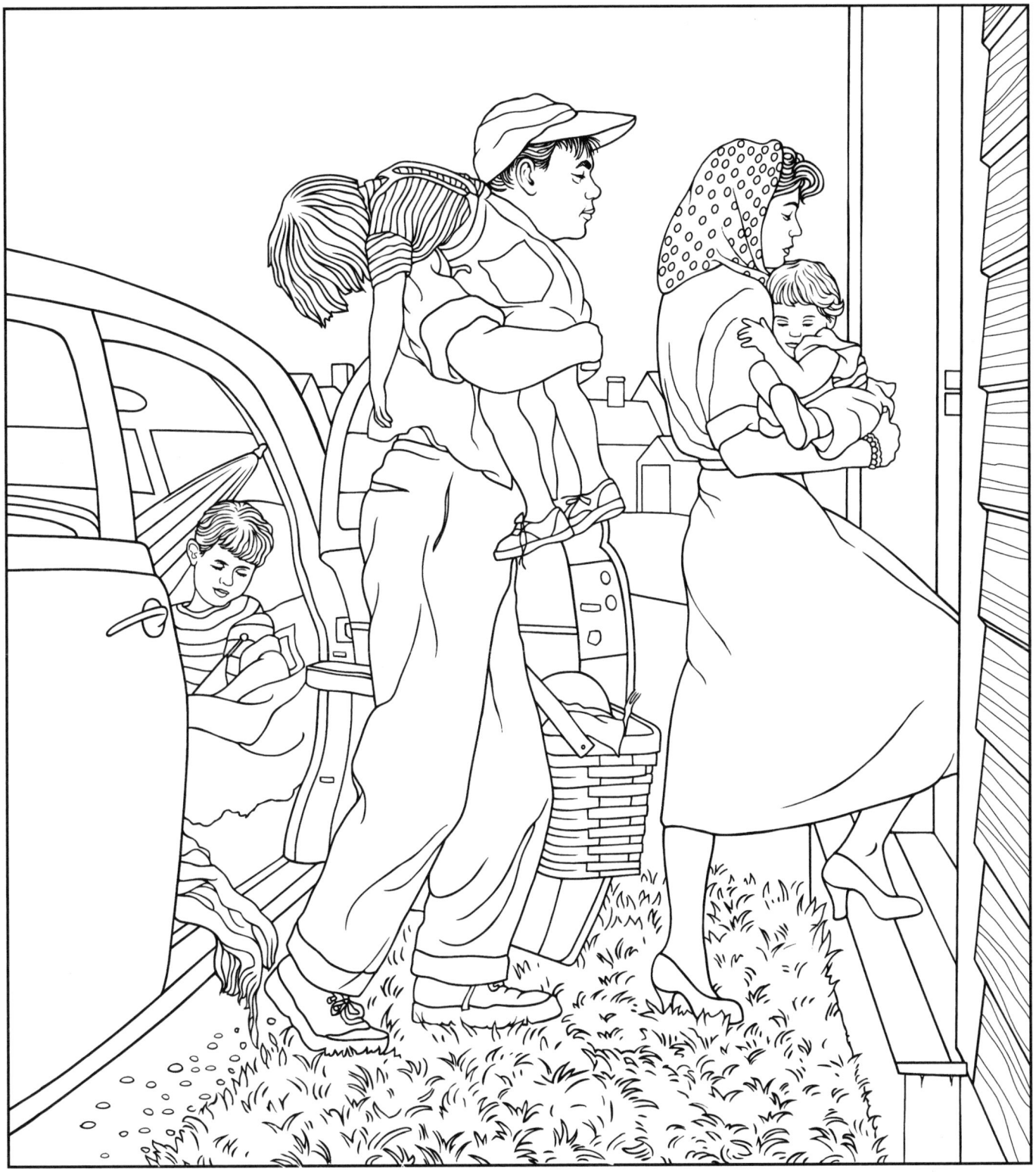

PLATE 9

Home at Last

George Hughes

Saturday Evening Post Cover, September 1, 1951

Illustration © SEPS. Licensed by Curtis Licensing, Indianapolis, IN.

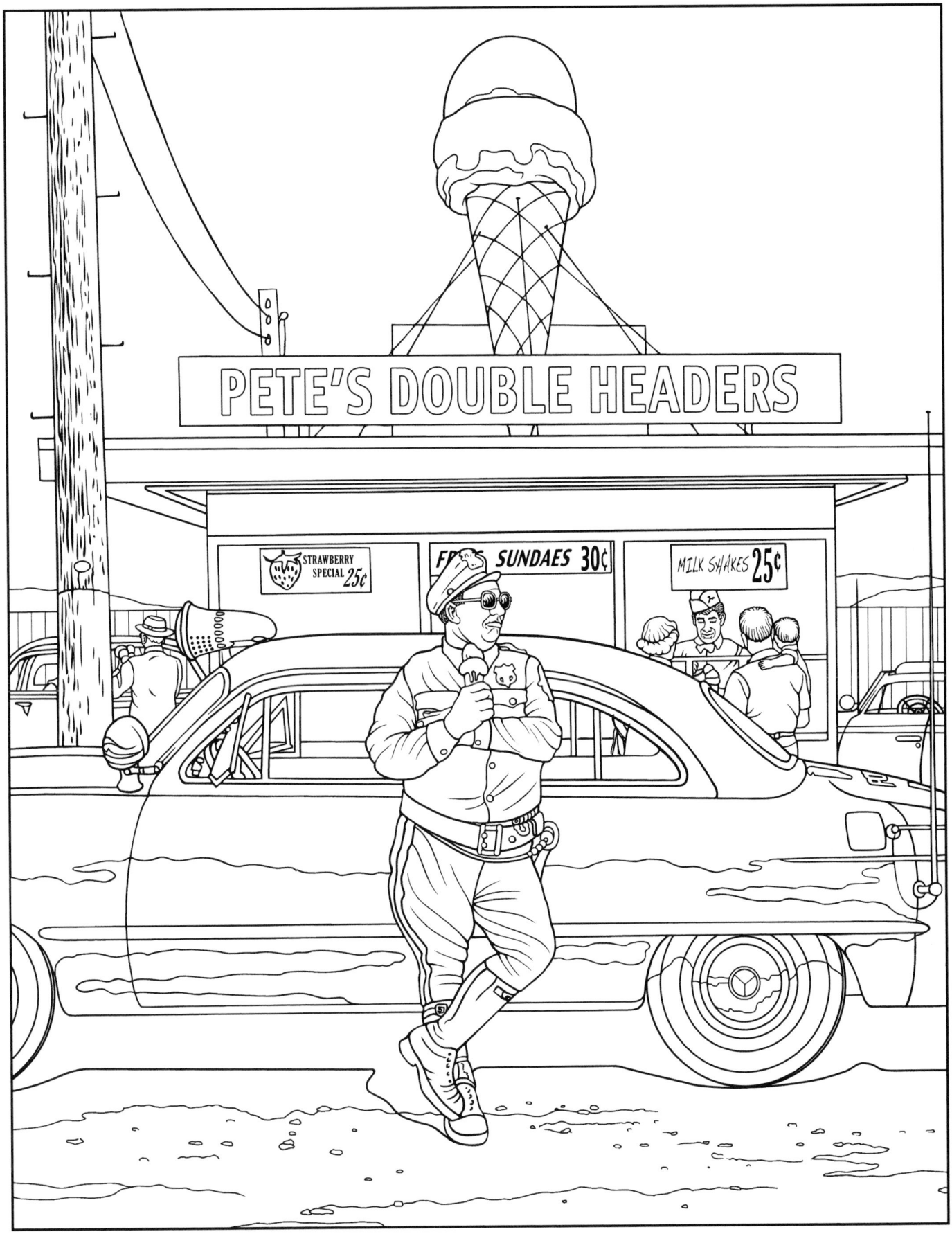
PETE'S DOUBLE HEADERS
STRAWBERRY SPECIAL 25¢
SUNDAES 30¢
MILK SHAKES 25¢

PLATE 10
Pete's Double Headers
Stevan Dohanos
Saturday Evening Post Cover, September 22, 1951
Illustration © SEPS. Licensed by Curtis Licensing, Indianapolis, IN.

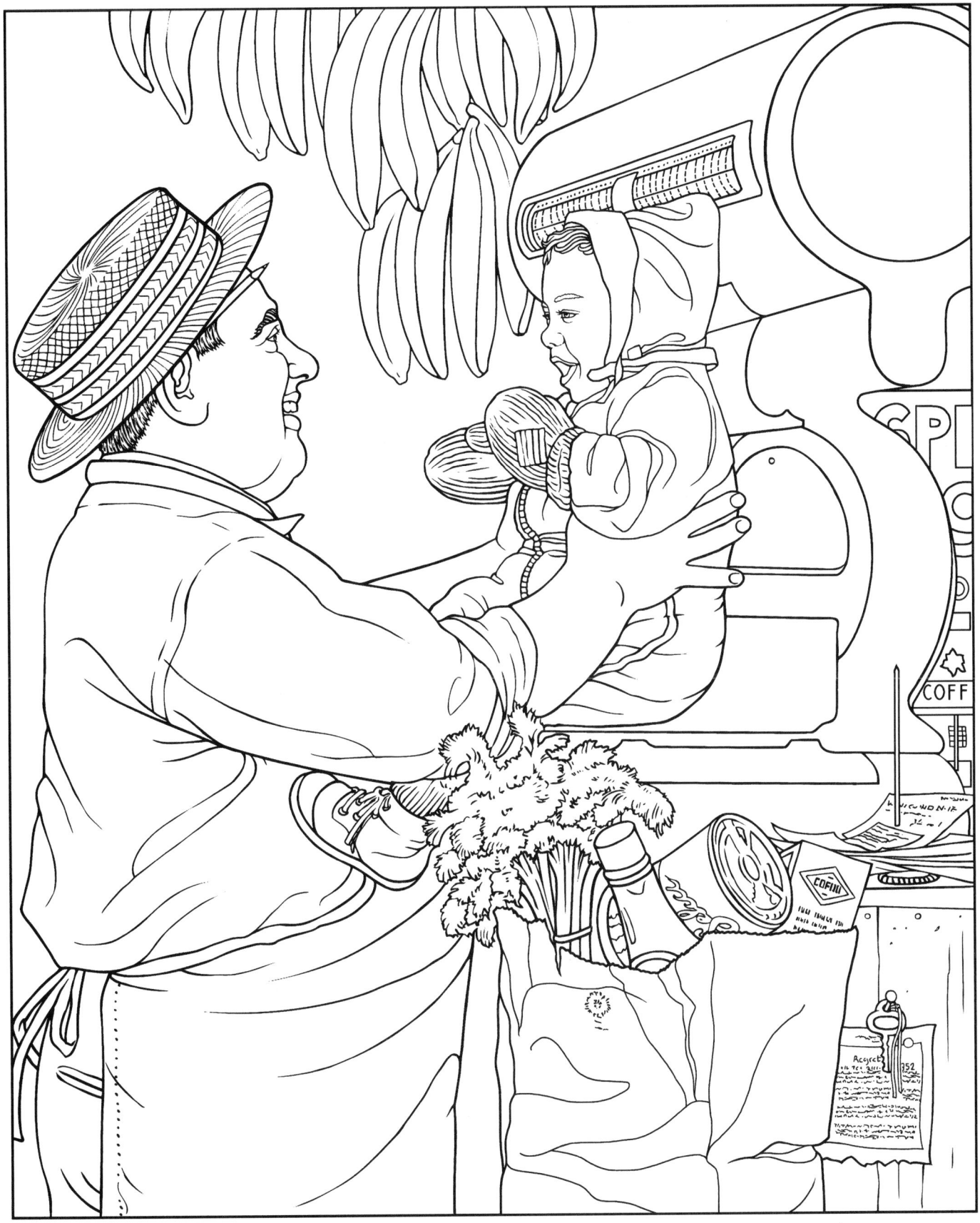
COFFI
Acquet
352

PLATE 11
Babies and Bananas
Stevan Dohanos
Saturday Evening Post Cover, April 5, 1952
Illustration © SEPS. Licensed by Curtis Licensing, Indianapolis, IN.

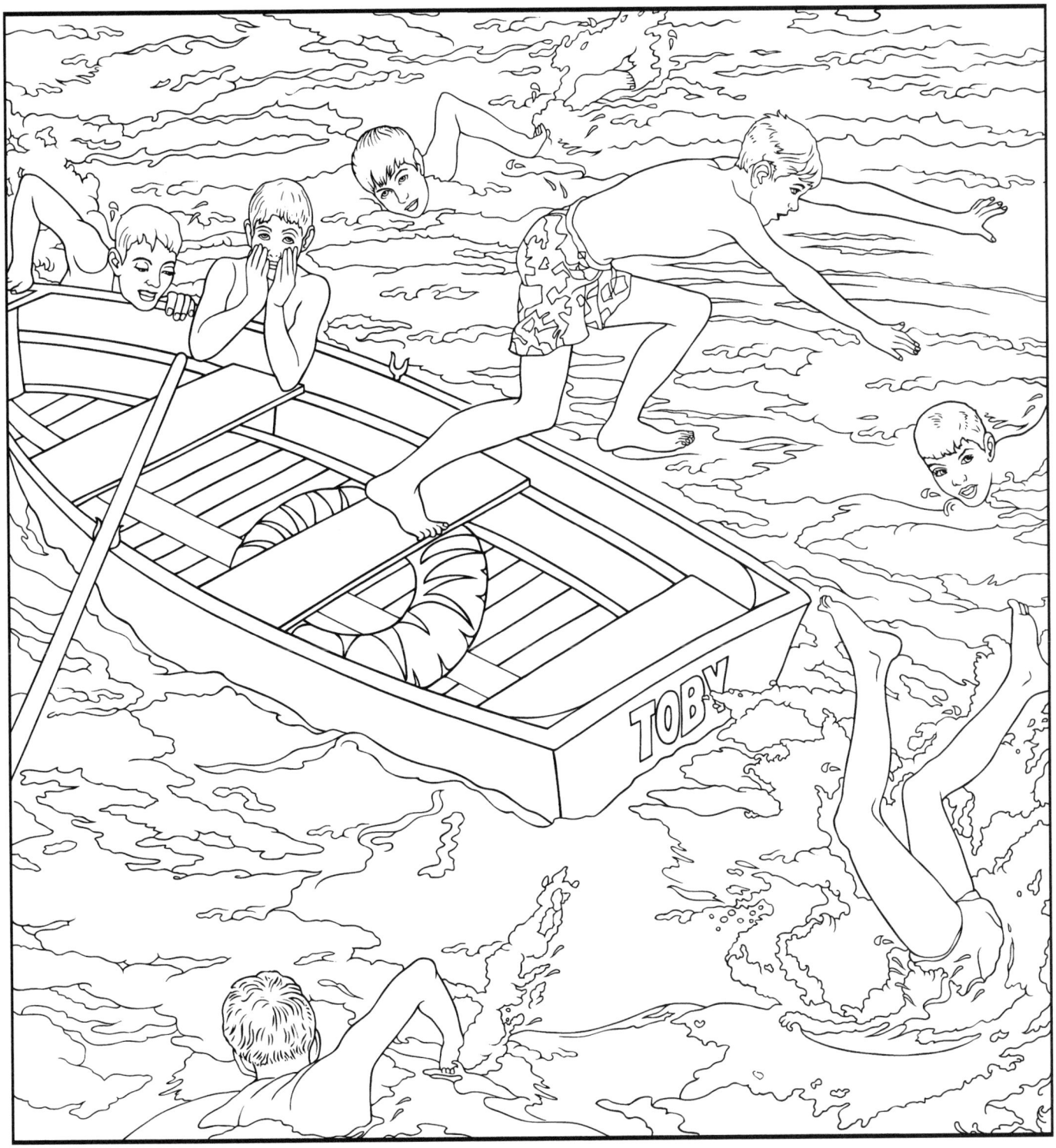
TOBY

PLATE 12
Rowboat Diving
Mead Schaeffer
Saturday Evening Post Cover, July 12, 1952
Illustration © SEPS. Licensed by Curtis Licensing, Indianapolis, IN.

NO
GIRLS
ALLOWED

PLATE 13
"No Girls Allowed"
Stevan Dohanos
Saturday Evening Post Cover, August 9, 1952
Illustration © SEPS. Licensed by Curtis Licensing, Indianapolis, IN.

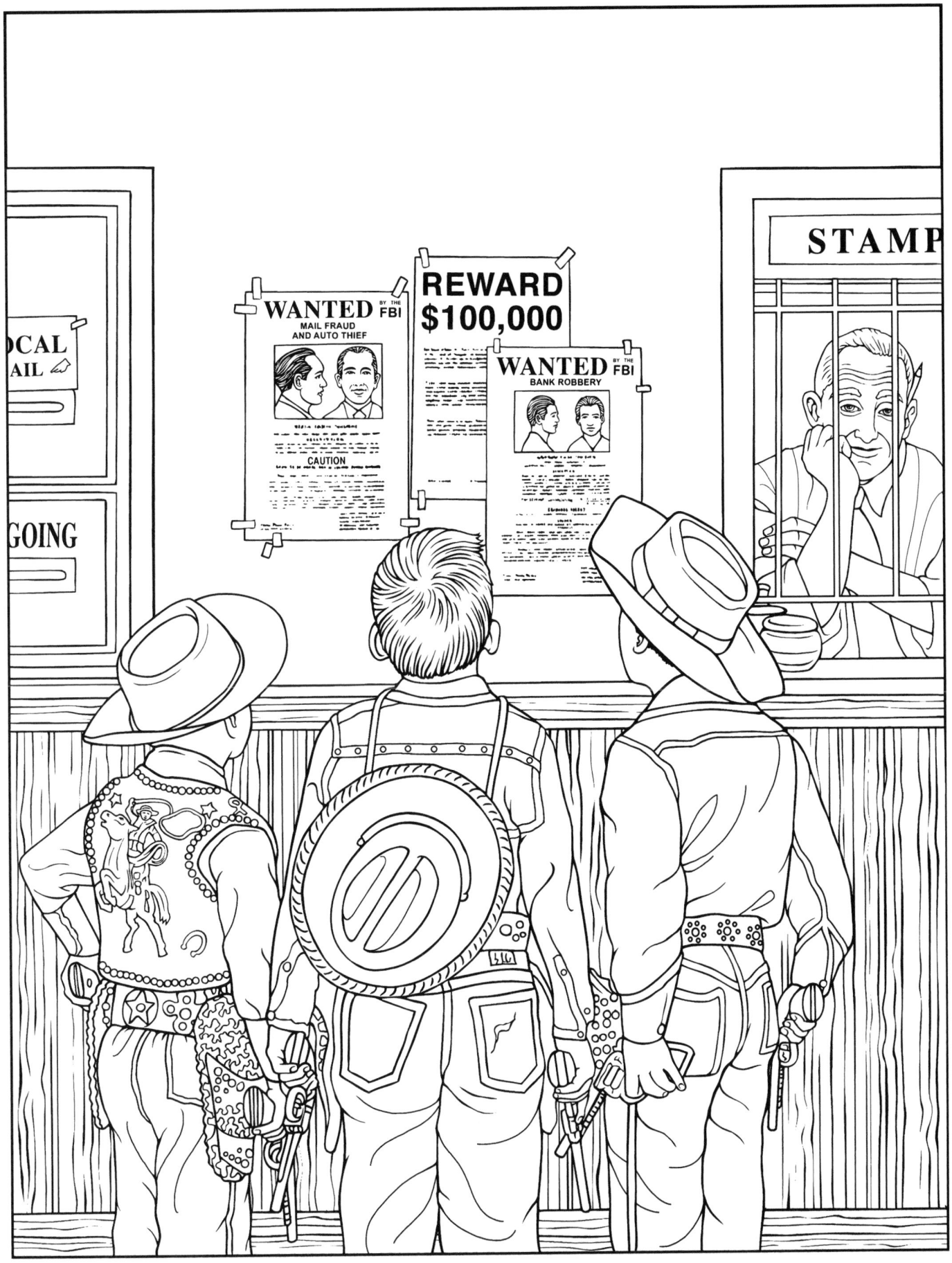
WANTED BY THE FBI
MAIL FRAUD
AND AUTO THIEF
CAUTION
REWARD
$100,000
WANTED BY THE FBI
BANK ROBBERY
STAMP
OCAL
AIL
GOING

PLATE 14
Wanted Posters
Stevan Dohanos
Saturday Evening Post Cover, February 21, 1953
Illustration © SEPS. Licensed by Curtis Licensing, Indianapolis, IN.

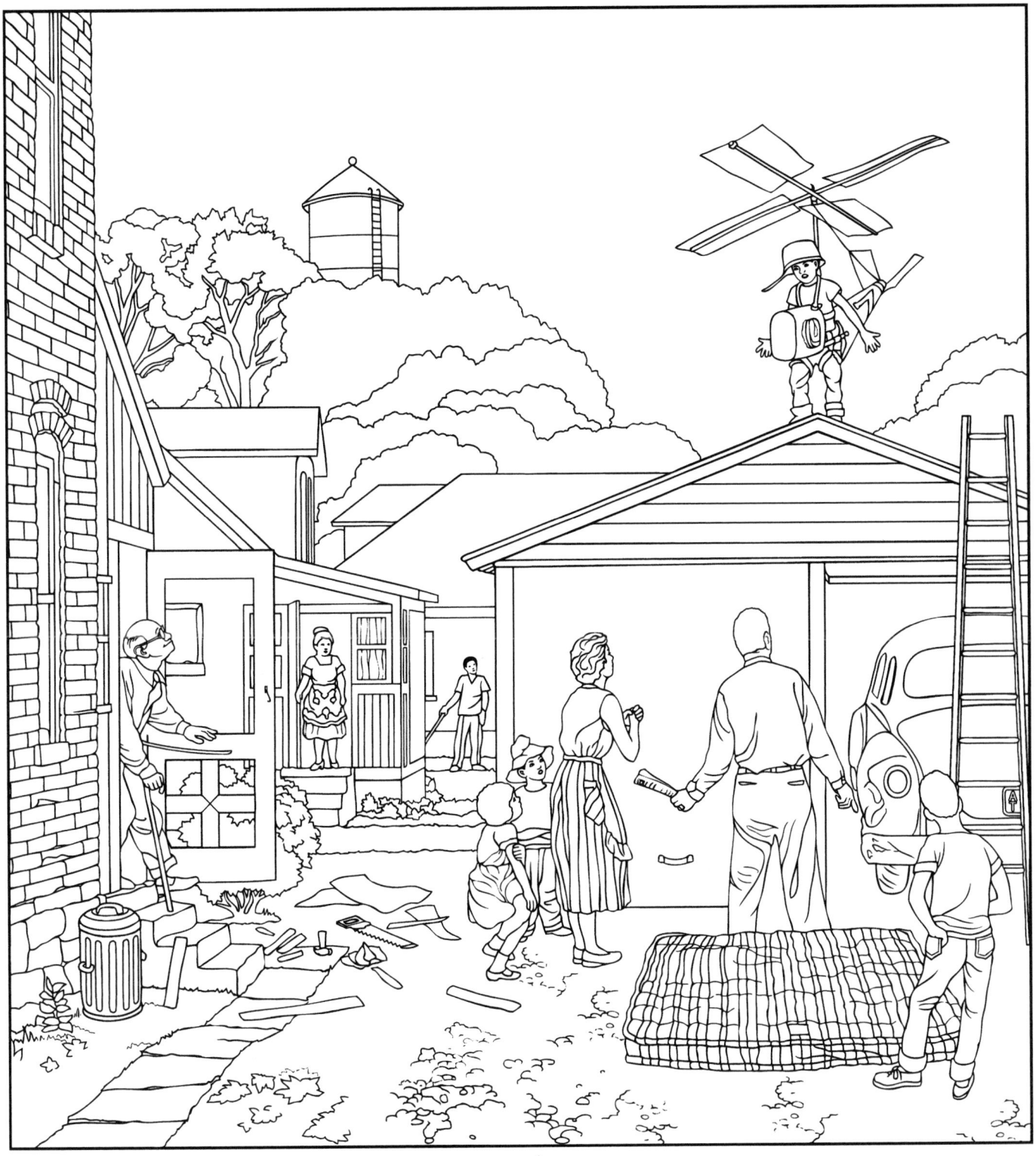

PLATE 15
Learning to Fly
John Falter
Saturday Evening Post Cover, June 20, 1953
Illustration © SEPS. Licensed by Curtis Licensing, Indianapolis, IN.

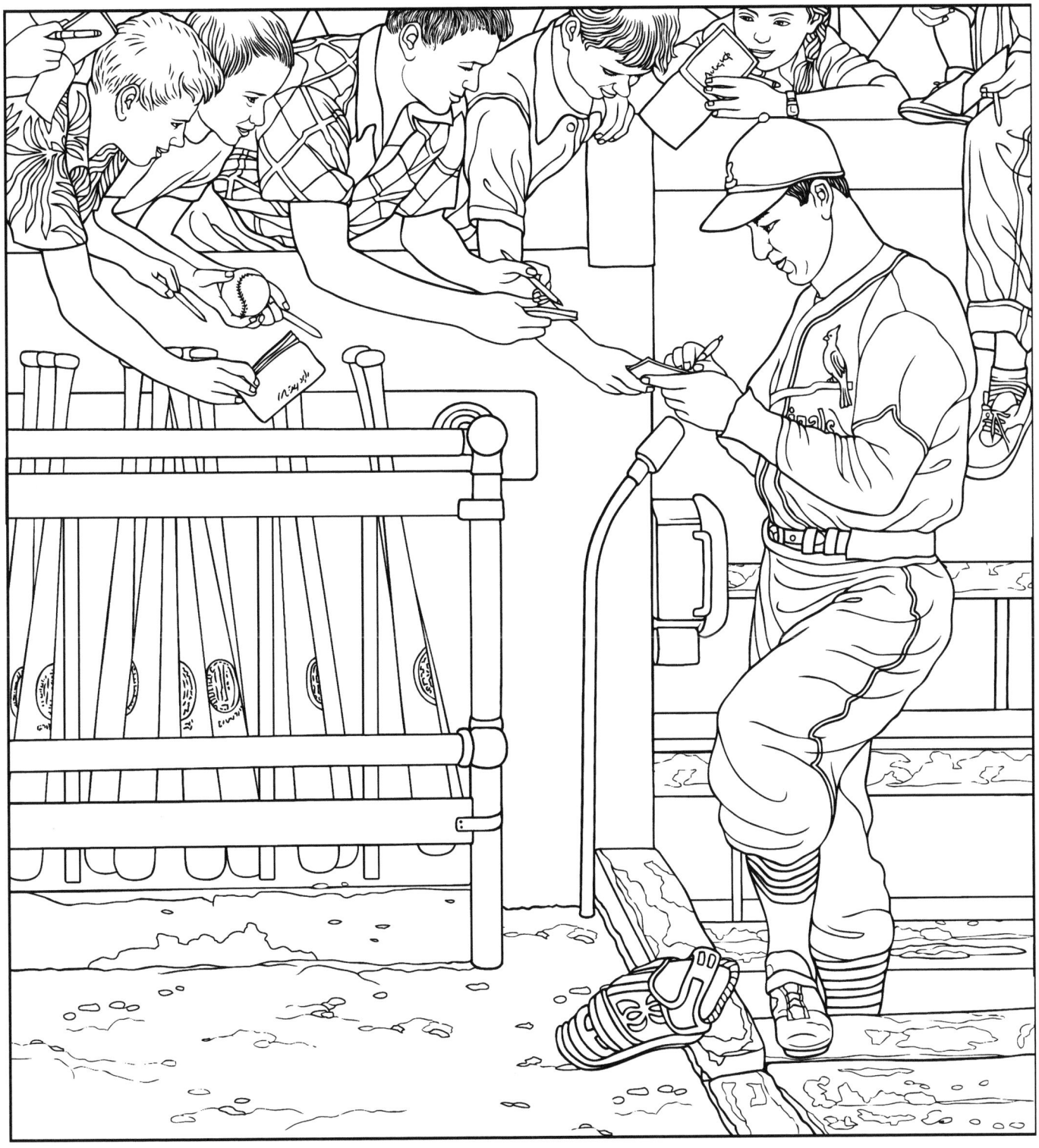

PLATE 16
"Stan the Man"
John Falter
Saturday Evening Post Cover, May 1, 1954
Illustration © SEPS. Licensed by Curtis Licensing, Indianapolis, IN.

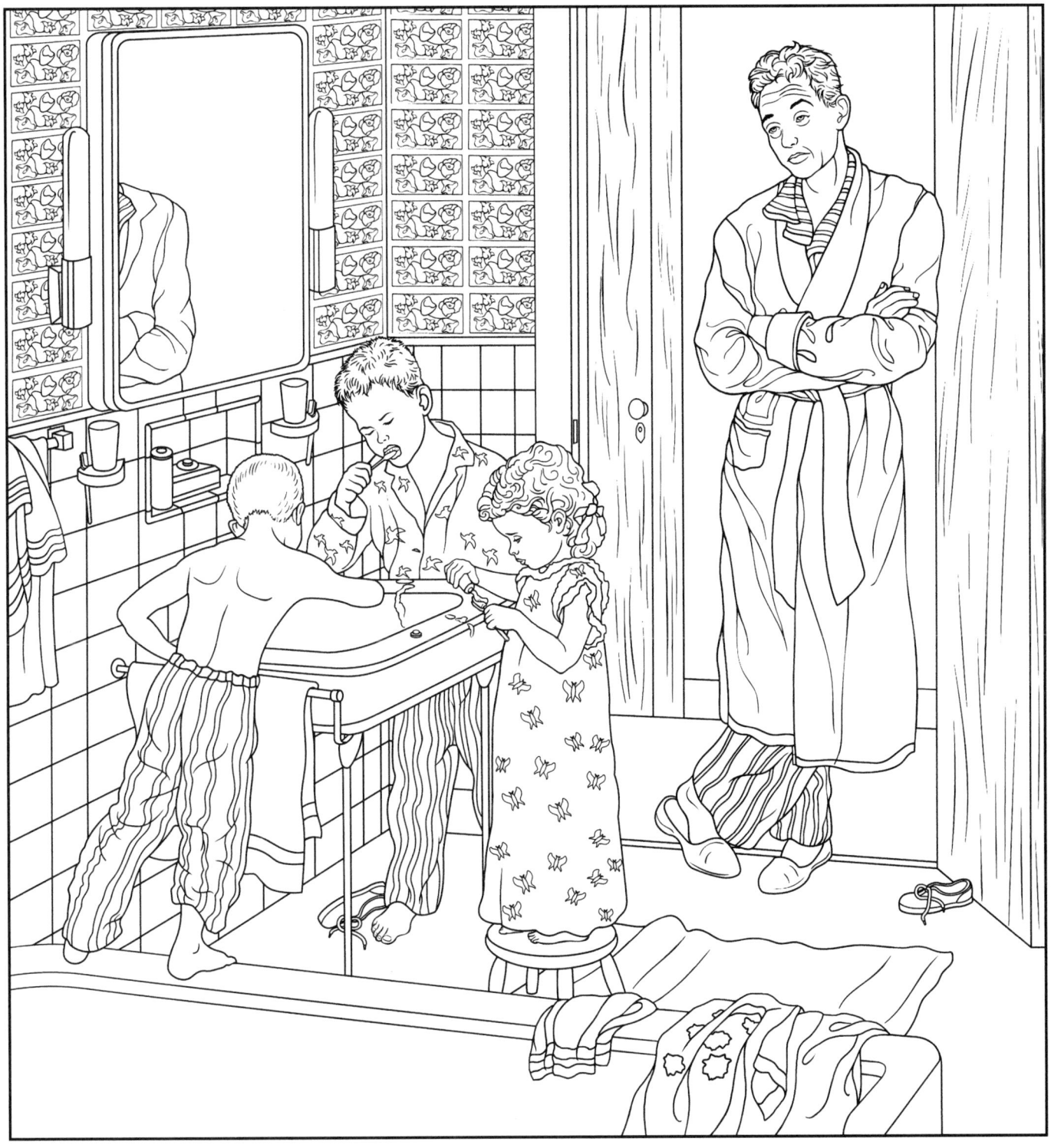

PLATE 17
Brushing Their Teeth
Amos Sewell
Saturday Evening Post Cover, January 29, 1955
Illustration © SEPS. Licensed by Curtis Licensing, Indianapolis, IN.

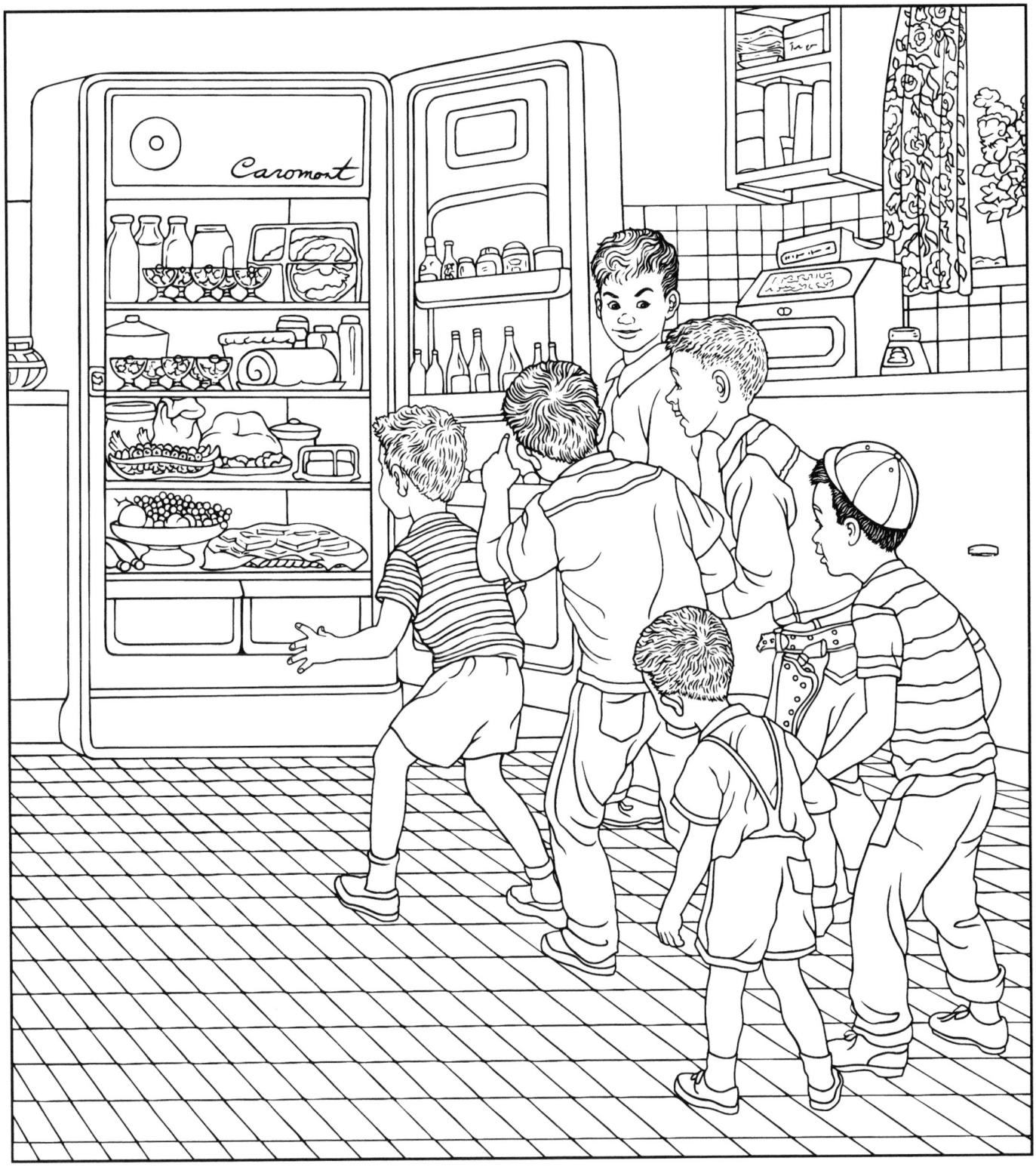
Caromont

PLATE 18
Refrigerator Raid
Amos Sewell
Saturday Evening Post Cover, February 19, 1955
Illustration © SEPS. Licensed by Curtis Licensing, Indianapolis, IN.

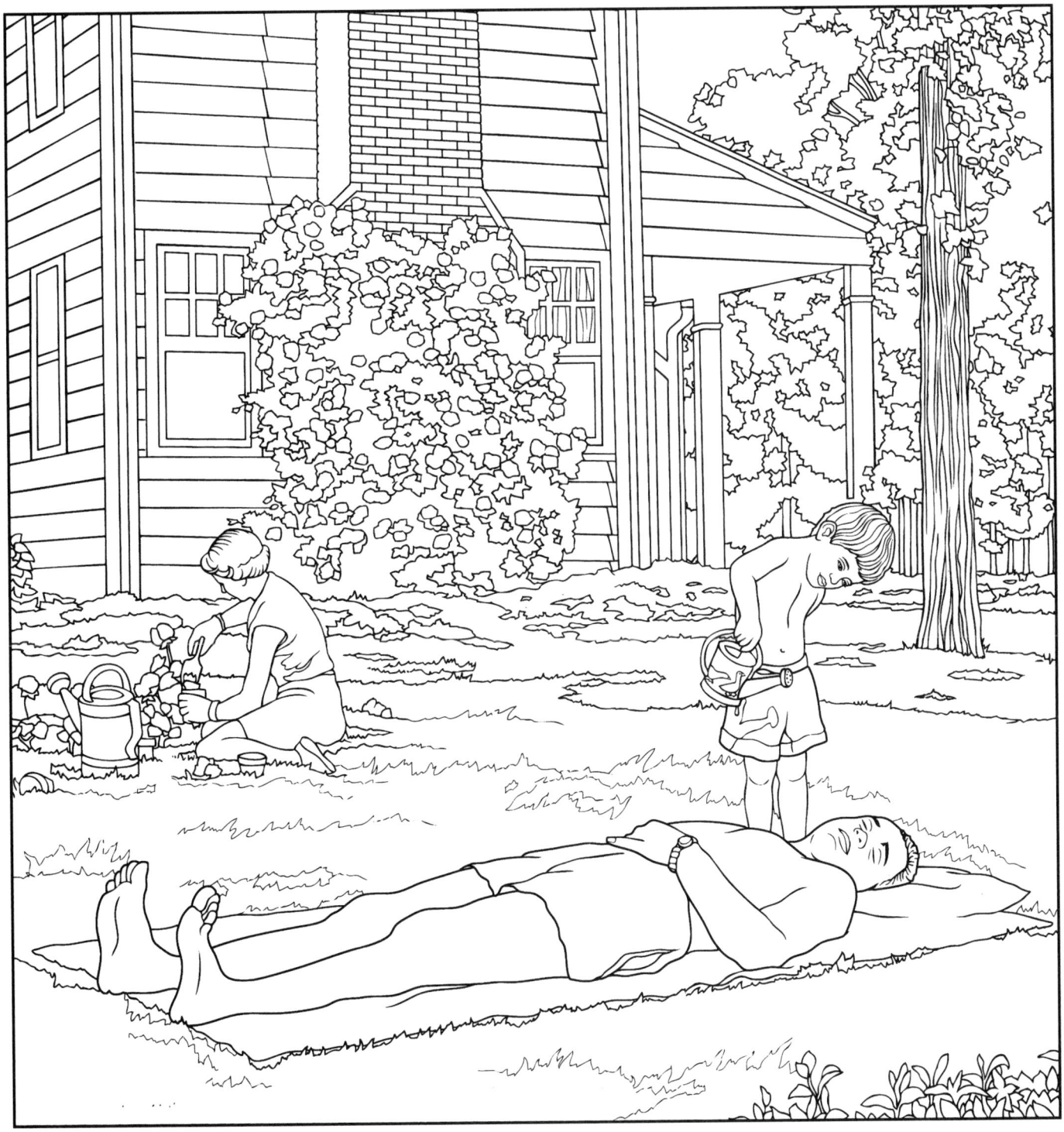

PLATE 19
Watering Father
Richard Sargent
Saturday Evening Post Cover, June 4, 1955
Illustration © SEPS. Licensed by Curtis Licensing, Indianapolis, IN.

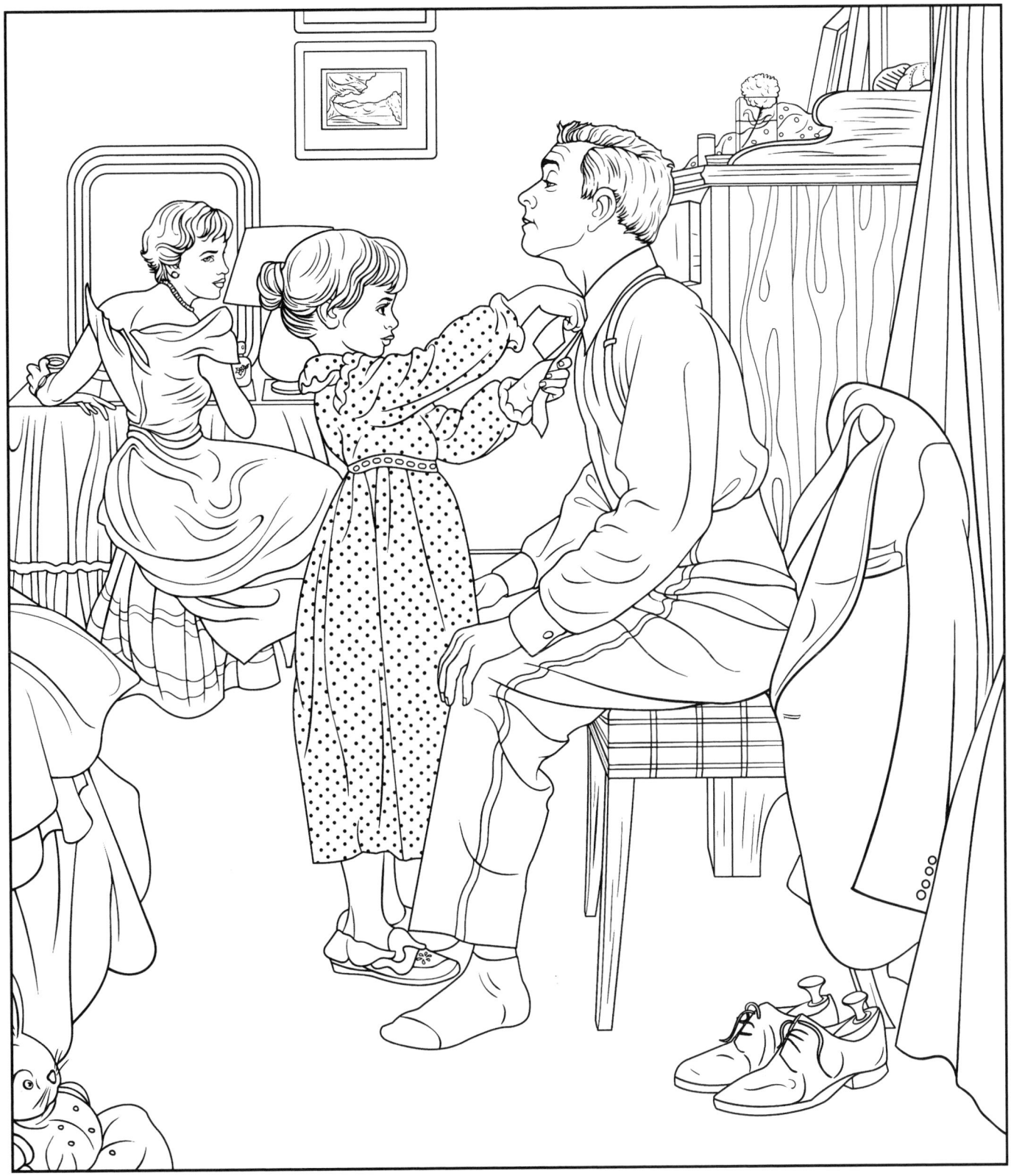

PLATE 20
Fixing Father's Tie
George Hughes
Saturday Evening Post Cover, December 31, 1955
Illustration © SEPS. Licensed by Curtis Licensing, Indianapolis, IN.

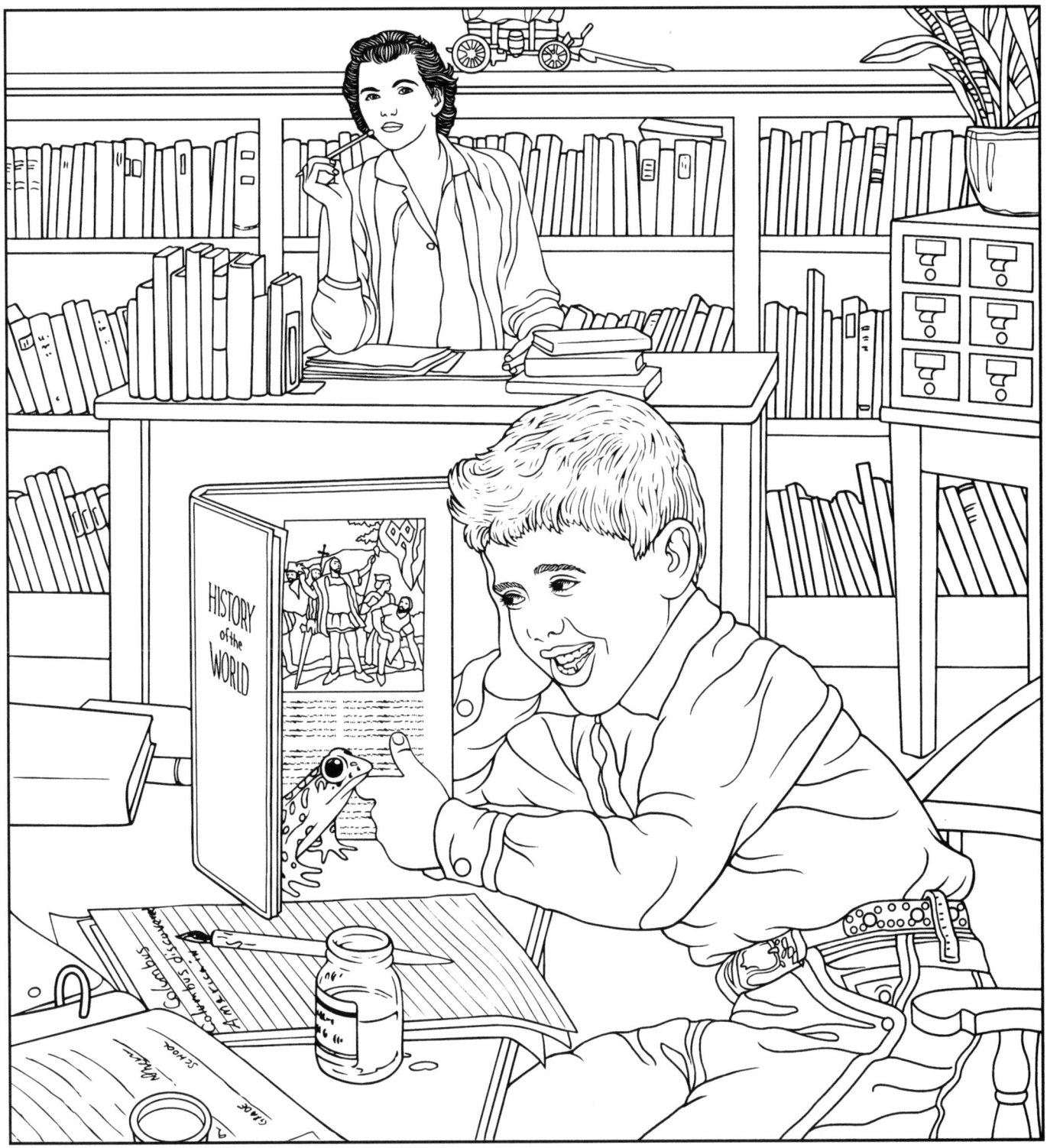
HISTORY
of the
WORLD

PLATE 21
Frog in the Library
Richard Sargent
Saturday Evening Post Cover, February 25, 1956
Illustration © SEPS. Licensed by Curtis Licensing, Indianapolis, IN.

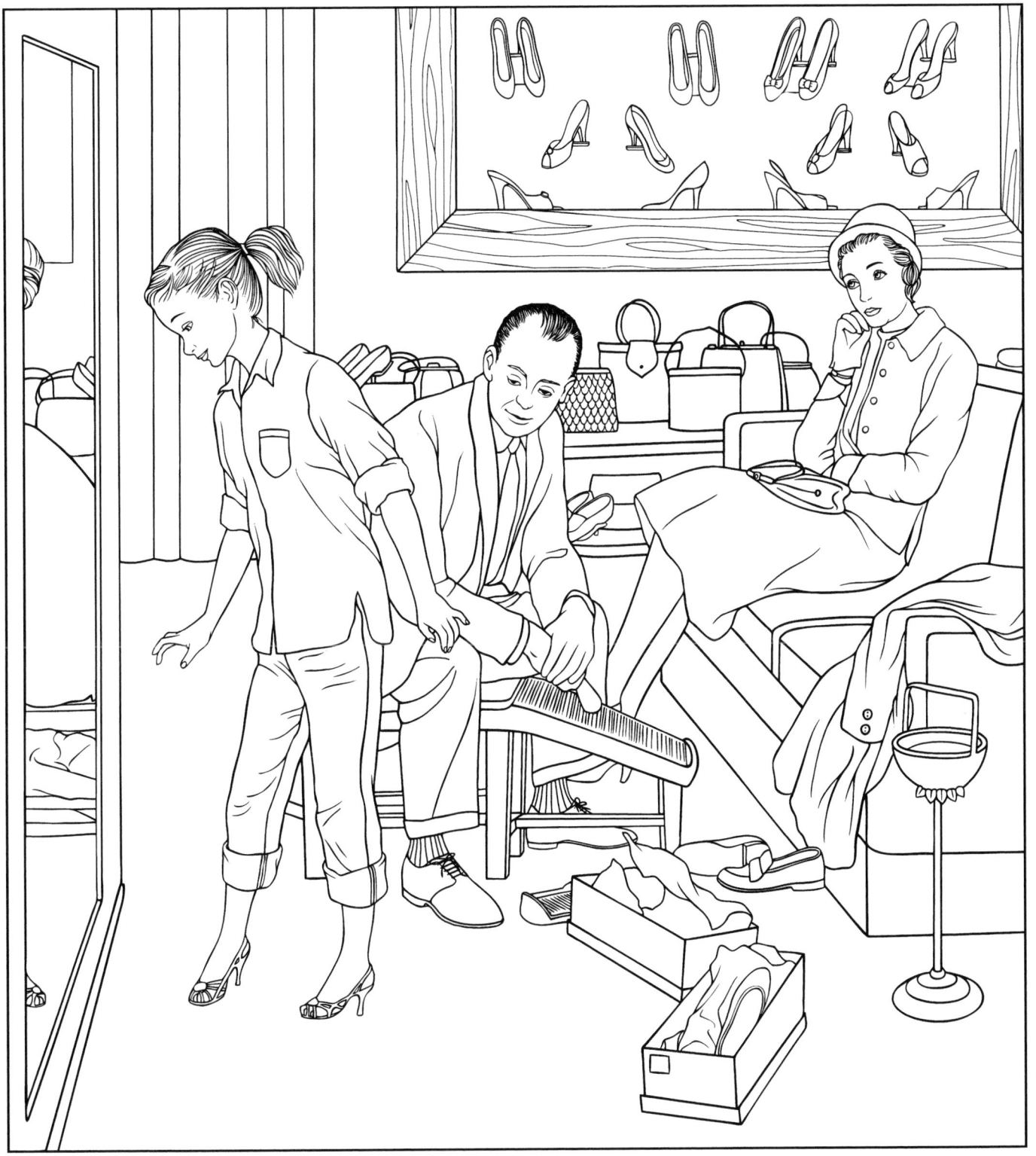

PLATE 22
First Pair of Heels
Amos Sewell
Saturday Evening Post Cover, March 31, 1956
Illustration © SEPS. Licensed by Curtis Licensing, Indianapolis, IN.

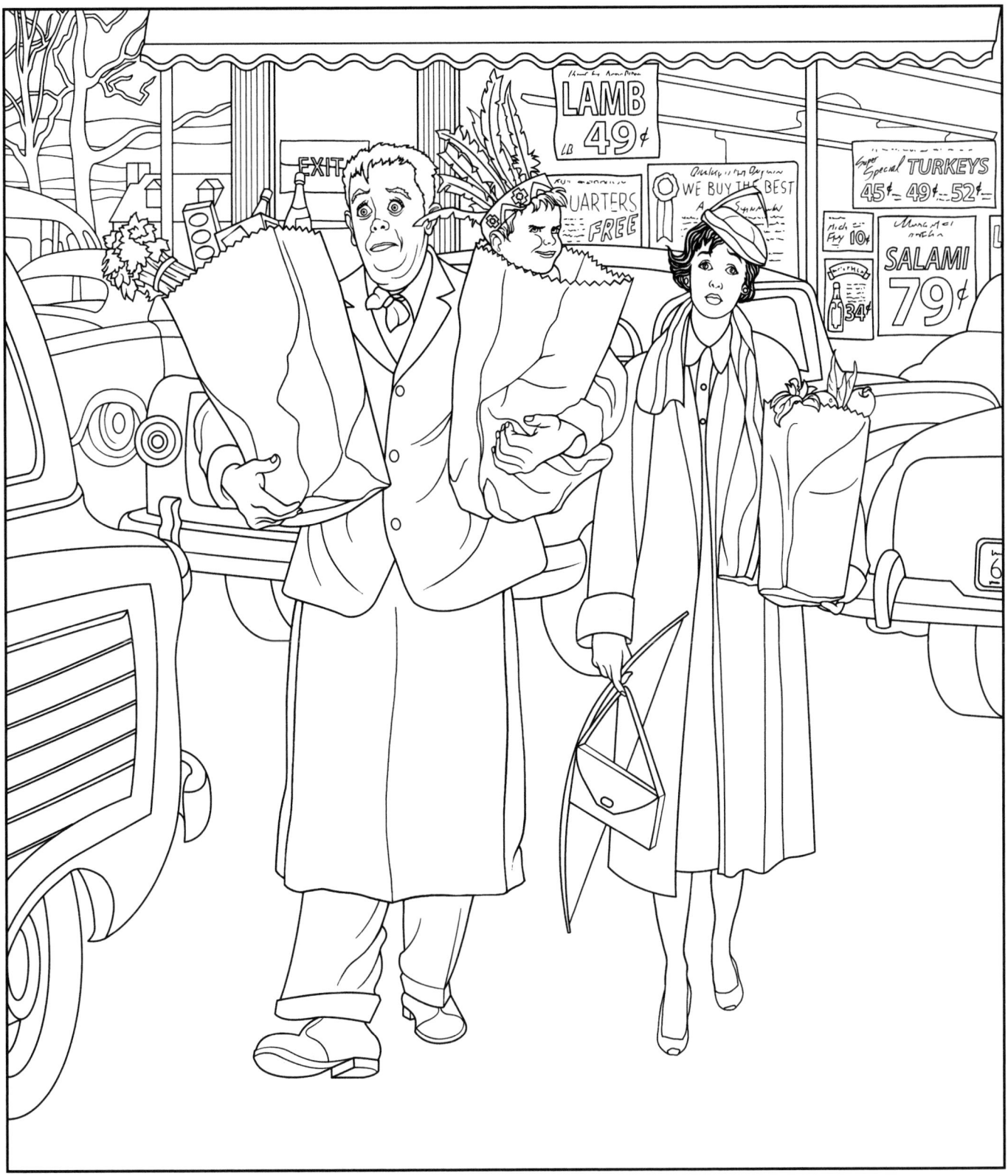
LAMB
LB 49¢
EXIT
QUARTERS
FREE
WE BUY THE BEST
TURKEYS
45¢ 49¢ 52¢
SALAMI
79¢
34¢

PLATE 23
Grocer with Bags
Richard Sargent
Saturday Evening Post Cover, April 14, 1956
Illustration © SEPS. Licensed by Curtis Licensing, Indianapolis, IN.

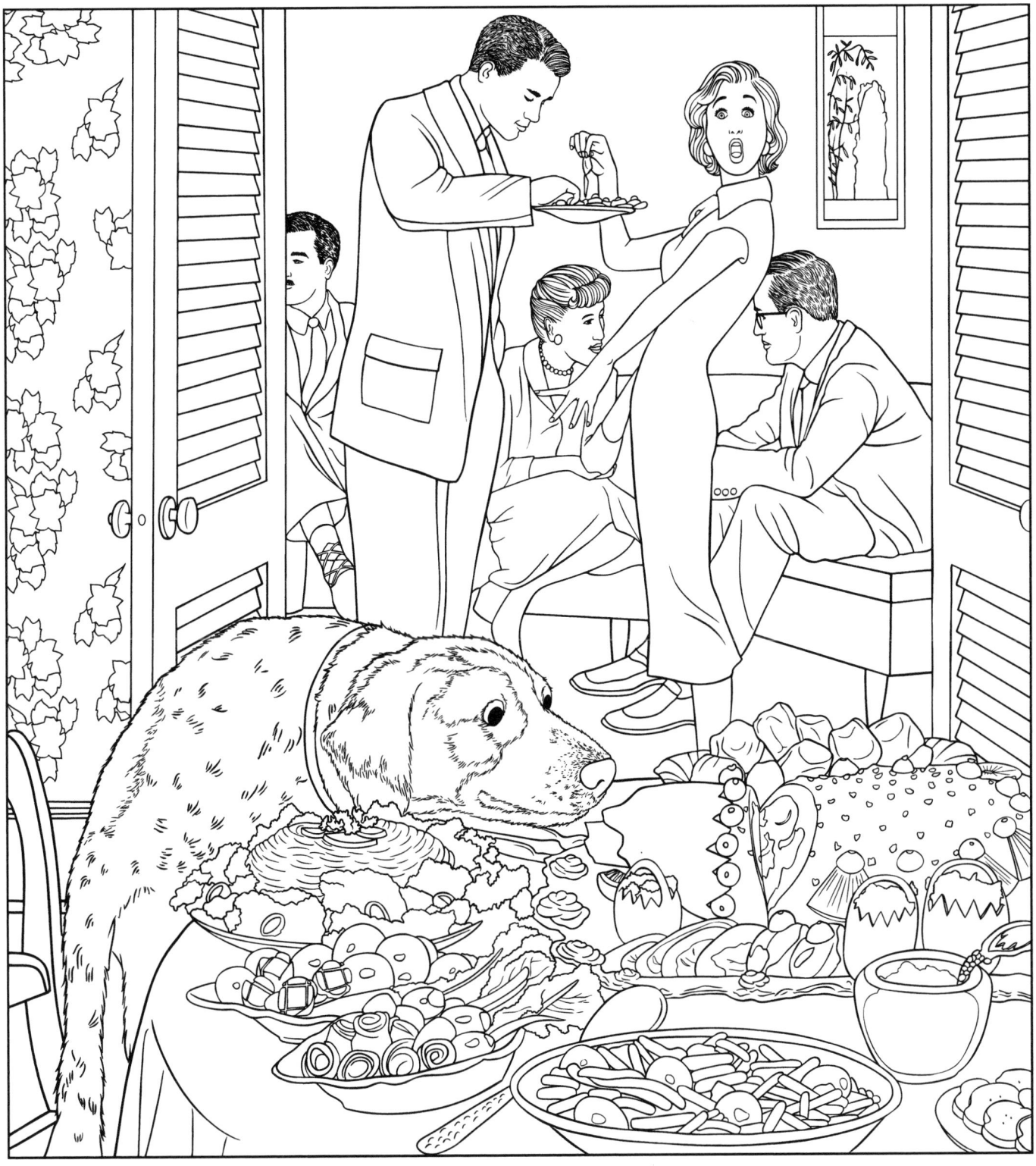

PLATE 24
Doggy Buffet
Richard Sargent
Saturday Evening Post Cover, January 5, 1957
Illustration © SEPS. Licensed by Curtis Licensing, Indianapolis, IN.

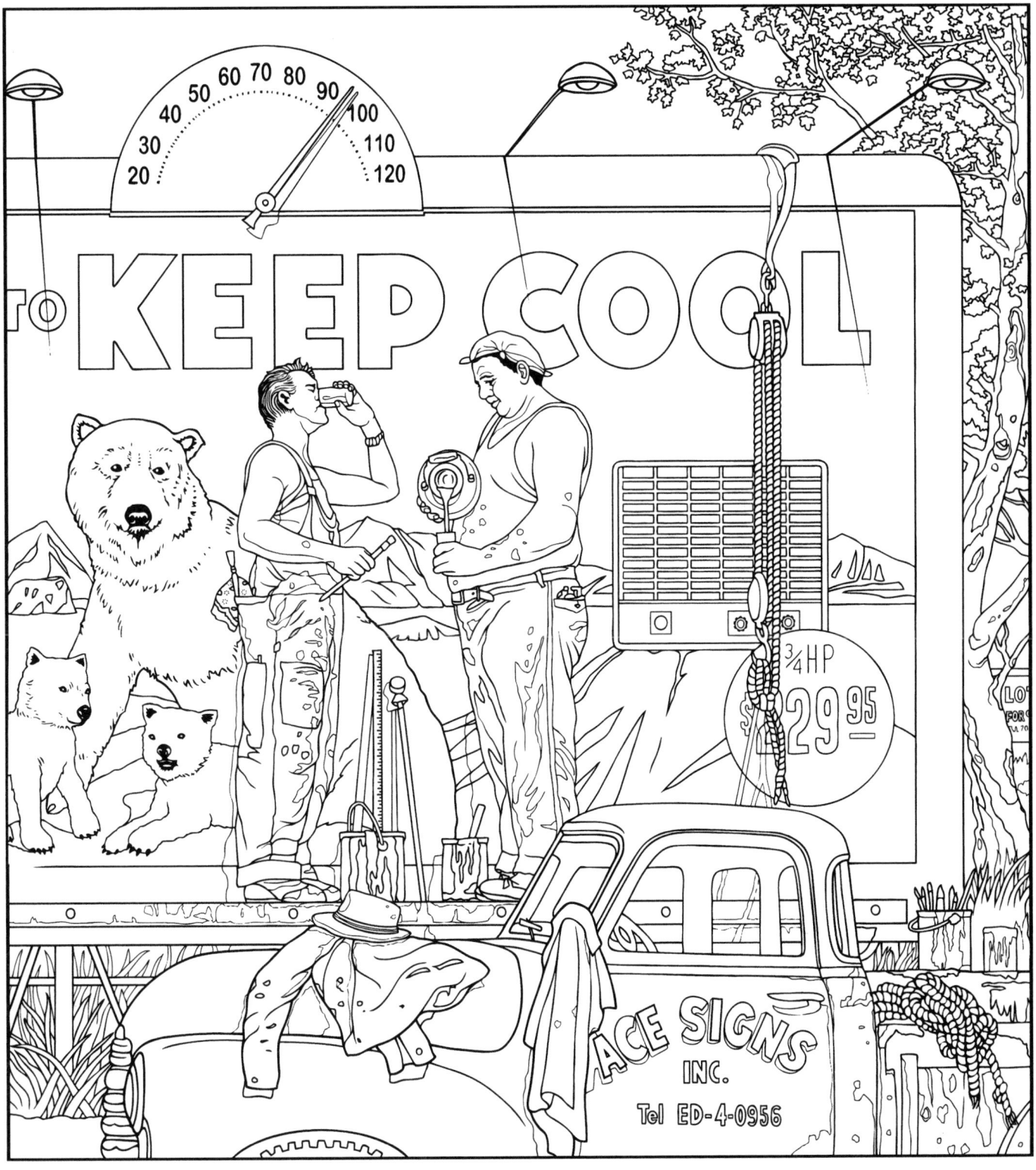
20 30 40 50 60 70 80 90 100 110 120
TO KEEP COOL
3/4 HP
$29.95
ACE SIGNS
INC.
Tel ED-4-0956

PLATE 25
Billboard Painters
Stevan Dohanos
Saturday Evening Post Cover, July 13, 1957
Illustration © SEPS. Licensed by Curtis Licensing, Indianapolis, IN.

THE FAY TERNACEY
Daily Pumpo
TIMES
SUN

PLATE 26
Sunscreen
Kurt Ard
Saturday Evening Post Cover, August 16, 1958
Illustration © SEPS. Licensed by Curtis Licensing, Indianapolis, IN.

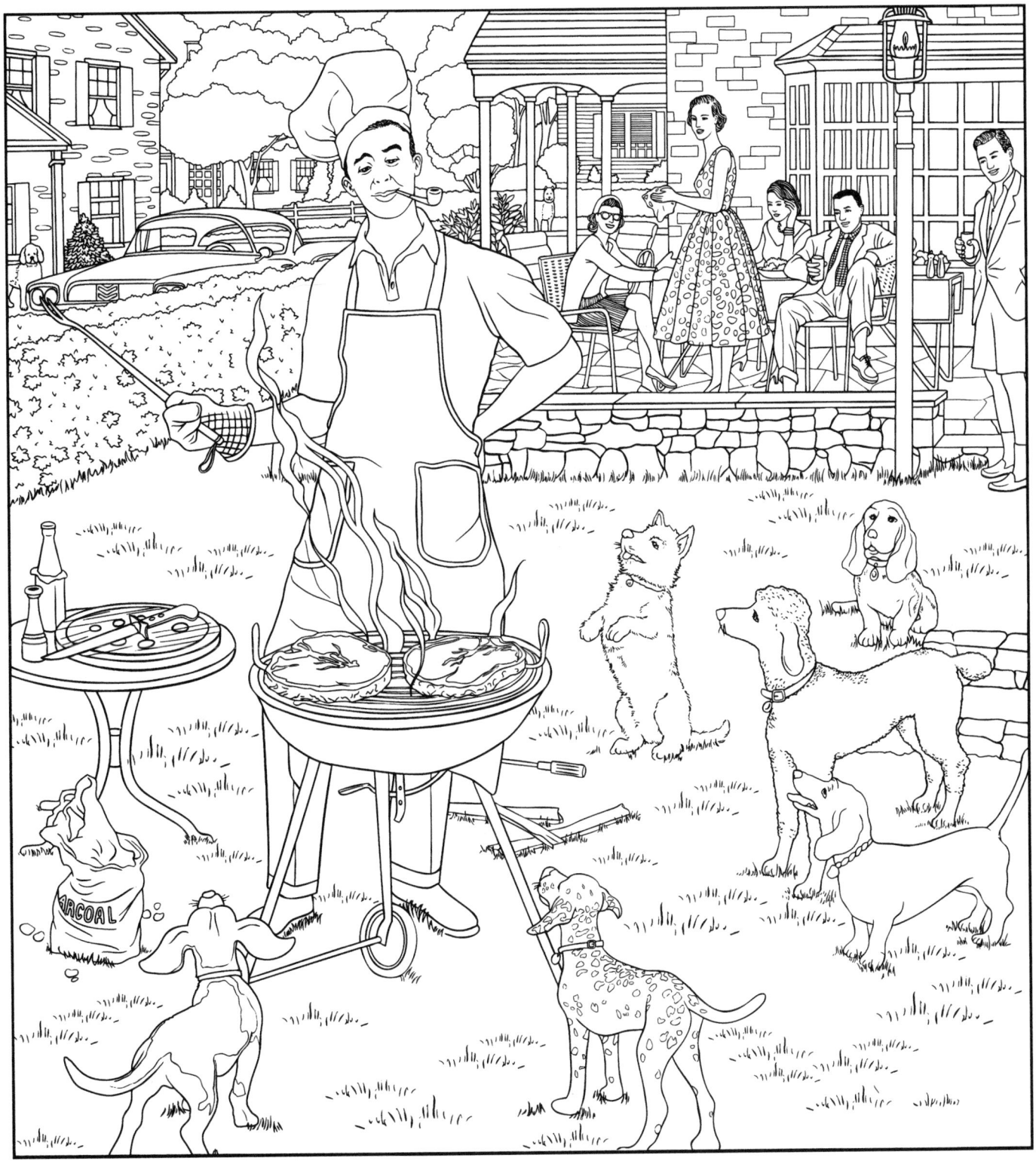
CHARCOAL

PLATE 27
Hot Dogs
Ben Kimberley Prins
Saturday Evening Post Cover, September 13, 1958
Illustration © SEPS. Licensed by Curtis Licensing, Indianapolis, IN.

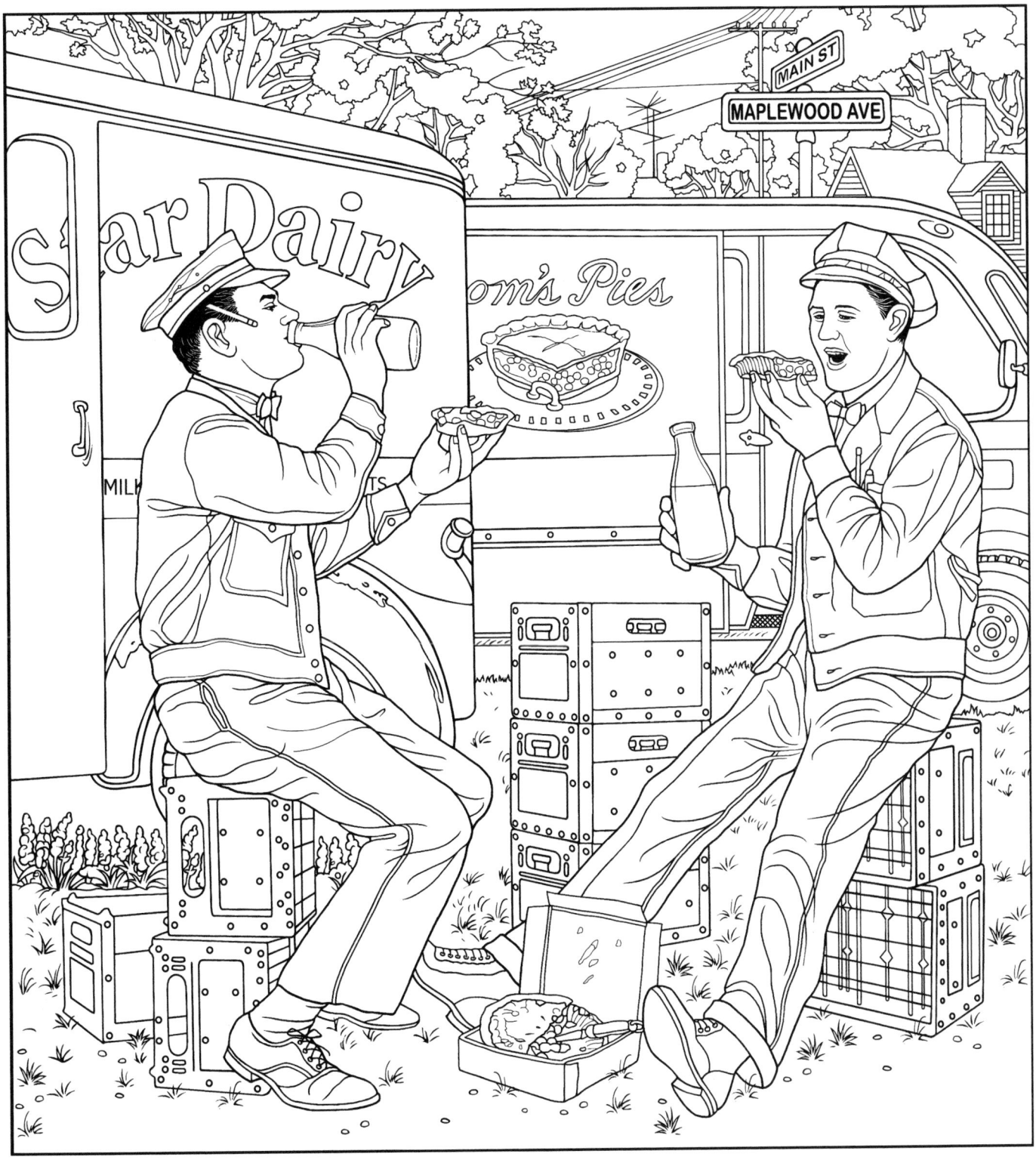
MAIN ST
MAPLEWOOD AVE
ar Dairy
om's Pies
MILK
TS

PLATE 28
Milkman Meets Pieman
Stevan Dohanos
Saturday Evening Post Cover, October 11, 1958
Illustration © SEPS. Licensed by Curtis Licensing, Indianapolis, IN.

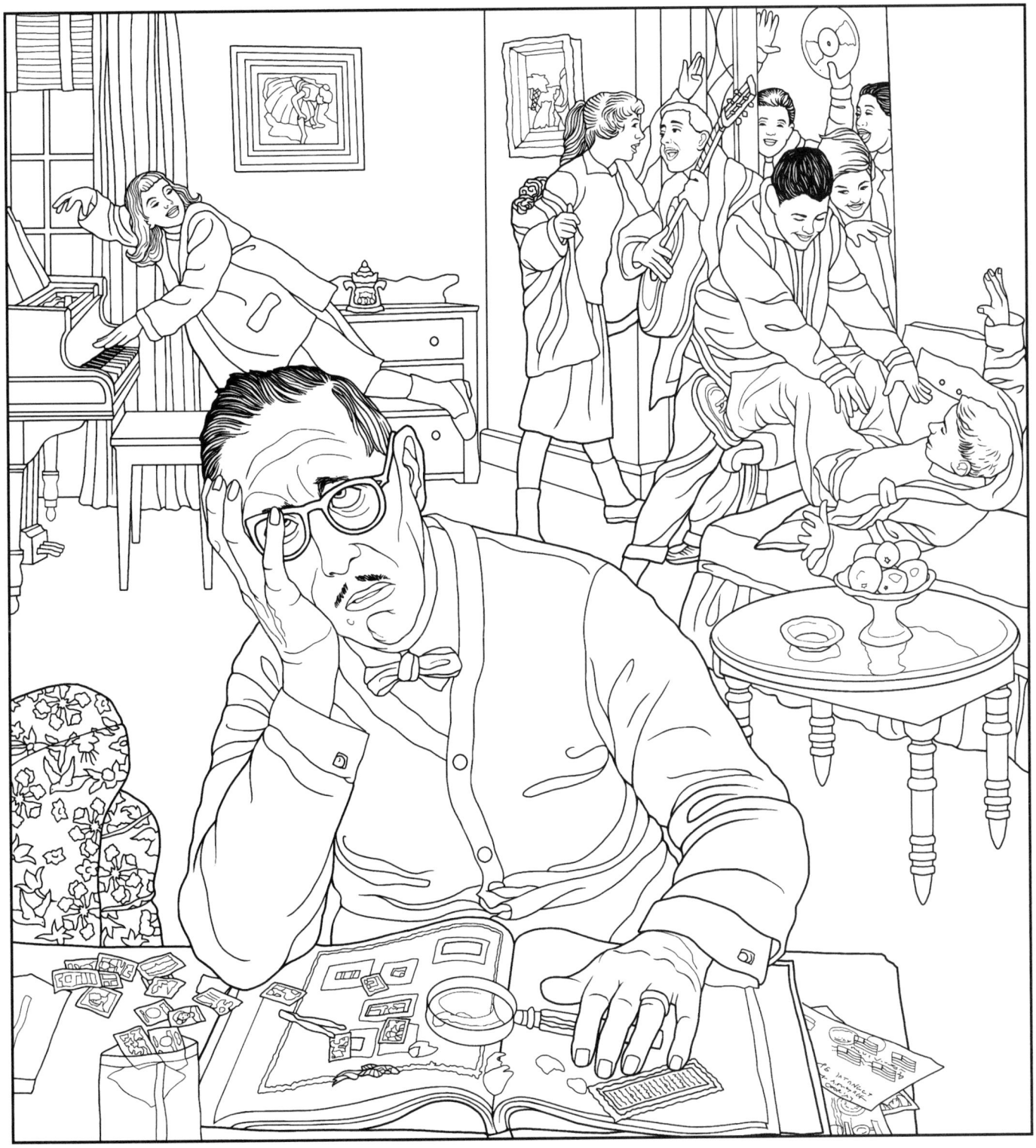

PLATE 29
No Quiet for Daddyo
Richard Sargent
Saturday Evening Post Cover, May 14, 1960
Illustration © SEPS. Licensed by Curtis Licensing, Indianapolis, IN.

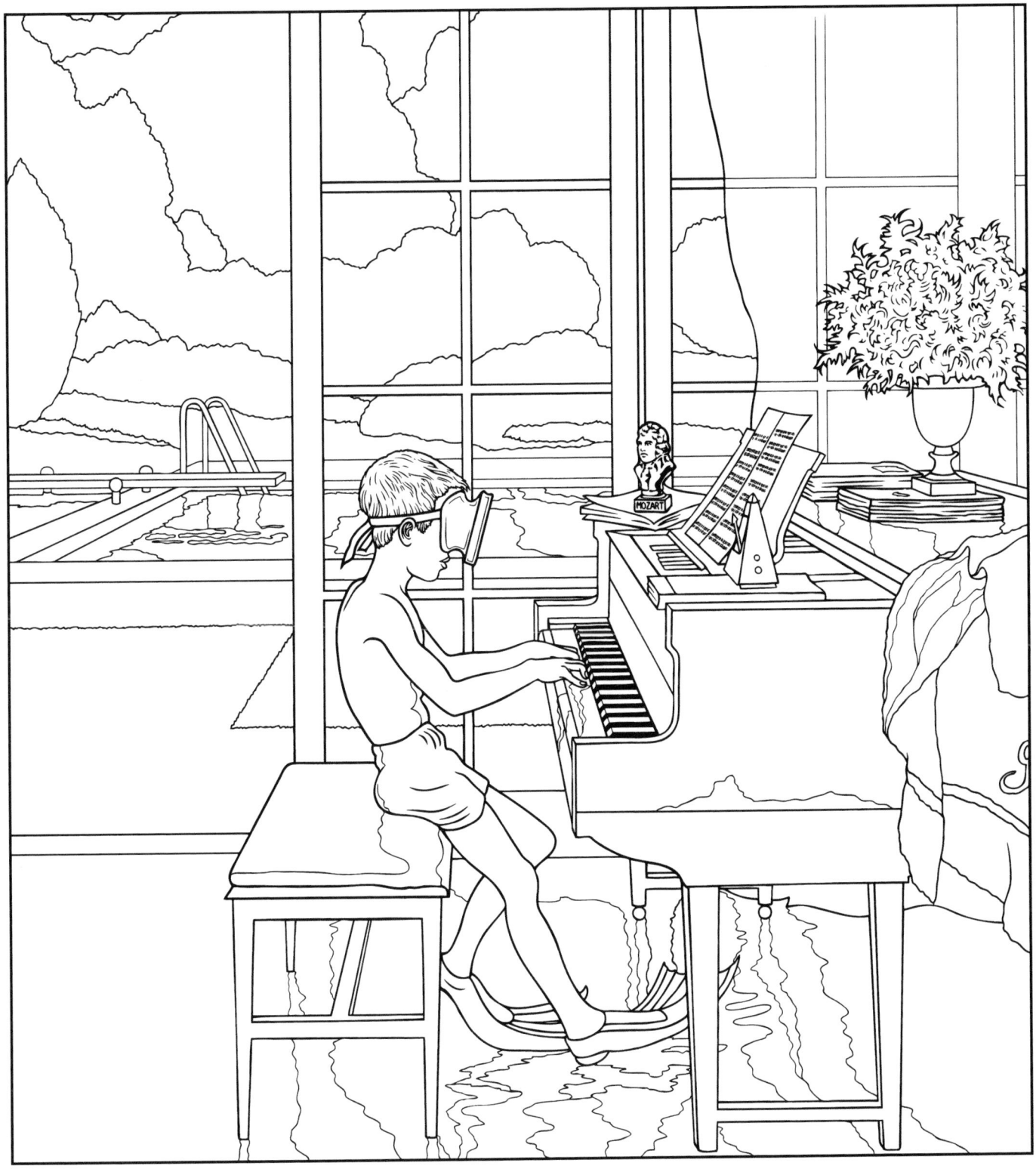
MOZART

PLATE 30
Poolside Piano Practice
George Hughes
Saturday Evening Post Cover, June 11, 1960
Illustration © SEPS. Licensed by Curtis Licensing, Indianapolis, IN.

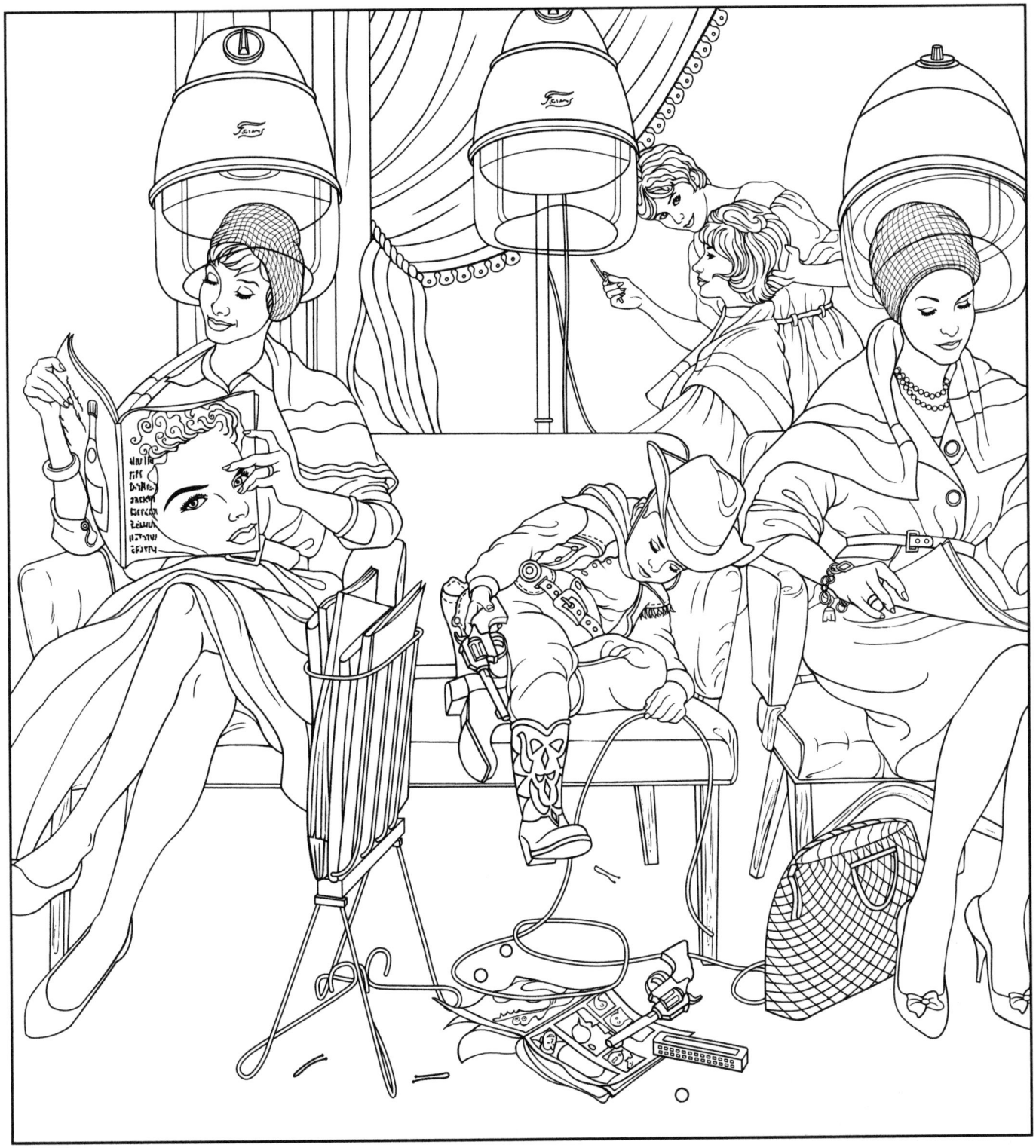

PLATE 31
Cowboy Asleep in Beauty Salon
Kurt Ard
Saturday Evening Post Cover, May 6, 1961
Illustration © SEPS. Licensed by Curtis Licensing, Indianapolis, IN.